COMING
—TO—
AMERICA
Immigrants from
EASTERN
EUROPE

SHIRLEY BLUMENTHAL

DELACORTE PRESS/NEW YORK

Published by
Delacorte Press
1 Dag Hammarskjold Plaza
New York, N.Y. 10017

Manufactured in the United States of America
First printing

Designed by Rhea Braunstein

Picture research by Paula McGuire

LIBRARY OF CONGRESS CATALOGING IN PUBLICATION DATA

Blumenthal, Shirley, [date of birth]
   Coming to America.

   Bibliography: p.
   Includes index.
   Summary: Discusses the reasons for the immigration of
Eastern Europeans to the United States in the late
nineteenth and early twentieth centuries and describes
the hardships, persecutions, and intolerable living
and working conditions that many had to endure until
they gained some measure of acceptance in their new
homeland.
   1. East European Americans—Juvenile literature.
2. United States—Emigration and immigration—Juvenile
literature. [1. East European Americans. 2. United
States—Emigration and immigration.] I. Title.
E184.E17B56   304.8′73′047   81–65503
ISBN 0–440–01468–9   AACR2

Contents

Introduction:
A New Immigration

"What then is the American?" asked Jean de Crèvecoeur in *Letters from an American Farmer,* the book that made him the literary celebrity of London after its publication there in 1782. Crèvecoeur's "letters" were really essays on American life. He had started writing them in 1774, when he was a farmer in the English colony of New York. Part of his answer to the question he set himself was:

> He is either an European or the descendent of an European, hence that strange mixture of blood, which you will find in no other country. I could point out to you a family whose grandfather was an Englishman, whose wife was Dutch, whose son married a French woman, and whose present four sons have now four wives of different nations. . . . Here individuals of all nations are melted into a new race.[1]

Crèvecoeur was the first of many commentators who would see the United States as a melting pot. But if the America of his time was a pot in which many nationalities simmered together, the stew had a decidedly English flavor. The colonies struggling for independence had been colonies of England. The English language, religion (Protestant), and codes (such as English Common Law) became the basis of American culture and politics. Today, we would describe this American climate as WASP— White, Anglo-Saxon*, Protestant.

Of course, as Crèvecoeur noted, other groups besides the English had settled in the Colonies. The main minorities were Scots, Germans, Dutch, Swedes, and French Huguenots, all Protestants, all from northern Europe.

Only two groups were different from the prevailing type: Jews and Irish Catholics. Since the Middle Ages, Jews had been despised and persecuted by the Christians of Europe for their "heretic" religion. And, since the Protestant Reformation, European Catholics and Protestants had mistrusted and warred with one another, each side claiming the truer faith. Religious prejudices crossed the ocean with the colonists, and, at first, Catholics and Jews faced discrimination in many of the colonies. Indeed, when the first group of Jewish immigrants

---

* Referring to the Germanic tribes who overran England in the fifth century; the term has since come to mean "English."

to America arrived in New Amsterdam in 1654, Governor Peter Stuyvesant wanted to throw them out. Only orders from Holland, one of the most tolerant countries in Europe, prevented him from doing so.

In the end, though, the growing American commitment to religious freedom won out over prejudice. This climate of religious tolerance, however, was maintained partly by the fact that, until well into the nineteenth century, there were not many Jewish and Catholic immigrants.

Americans, then, in their first century as a nation, were people fused from Old World people who had much in common. Until about 1880, the majority of immigrants continued to come from northern Europe. And the United States was wide open to receive them; a land that spanned a continent needed people to develop it. Most of these immigrants became farmers in the Midwest where land was cheap. There was space enough and opportunity for hard-working newcomers to prosper as they helped their communities grow. These "old immigrants" fit in and made do fairly well.

Americans got their first taste of a new kind of immigrant in the five-year period of 1846 through 1850, when a million and a half people fleeing famine and plague arrived from Ireland. Oppressed for centuries by English rulers, the Irish were uneducated and unskilled, and now they were starving. They had barely the resources to make it to the port cities of New York and Boston, much less to go on from there to the open stretches of the Midwest. They had to take low-paying, dirty, physically exhausting jobs, which earned them the scorn of more affluent Americans. And they were Catholic.

The Protestant hostility to Catholics had stayed below the surface as long as there weren't many Catholics in the United States. But now, Irish Catholics seemed to be taking over the northeastern cities where, in poverty and ignorance, they filled decaying tenements, cellars, and shanties. They became the country's first urban slum-dwellers, and "older" Americans regarded them as dirty, drunken, and undesirable. Anti-Catholic sentiment began to be heard. As the century progressed, more and more immigrants came from the non-Protestant countries of Europe. In time, anti-Catholic sentiment would be enlarged to cover the entire "new immigration."

The "new immigrants" from eastern Europe started to arrive in large numbers in the 1870s along with southern Europeans such as the Italians and Greeks. The eastern group consisted of Poles, Slovaks, Czechs, Hungarians, Ukrainians, Russians, Croats, Lithuanians, Serbs, Slovenes, Bulgarians, Macedonians, Dalmatians, Armenians, Romanians, and Jews. Except for the Jews, who were not allowed to own or lease land in much of Europe, most of these immigrants were peasants, or farmers. Many of them had been freed just fifteen or twenty years earlier from serfdom, under which their land and their labor had been the property of landlords. They came from small villages, where life had not changed for centuries. Many could not read or write, and those who could had little other learning. They were dreadfully poor. A few had had industrial experience in the mines and factories that were just beginning to appear in eastern Europe. But for the most part, the agricultural and industrial revolutions that were thrusting the nations of northern Europe into modern times had not yet reached their countries.

The new immigrants were able to get only the lowest-paying jobs in the mines and factories of America. They lived in the oldest, most run-down, dirty, crowded quarters of the cities. They looked different from northern Europeans—shorter, with darker coloring—and their languages and customs seemed strange. Their religions were the older ones that Protestants regarded with suspicion; they were Jews, Catholics, and members of the Eastern Orthodox Church.

Most alarming were their numbers. Between 1870 and 1924, some eight million immigrants came to America from eastern Europe. At the same time, about five million arrived from Greece and Italy. (The total U.S. population rose from 62.9 million in 1890 to 105.7 million in 1920.) They concentrated in the cities and industrial towns of the Northeast and Midwest and seemed to inundate them.

What now was the American? The following

description of the mingling of Old World peoples in the New World, written in 1902, is a far cry from the optimistic account of Jean de Crèvecoeur:

> But now there came multitudes of men of lowest class from the south of Italy and men of the meaner sort out of Hungary and Poland, men out of the ranks where there was neither skill nor energy nor any initiative of quick intelligence; and they came in numbers which increased from year to year, as if the countries of the south of Europe were disburdening themselves of the more sordid and hapless elements of their population.[2]

Ten years later the man who wrote this, Woodrow Wilson, would become President of the United States. Wilson expressed the thoughts of many who saw the country changing and who didn't like the shape of the future.

At the end of the nineteenth century the American frontier was closing. Land was no longer cheap. Industrialization was transforming the ways in which people worked. The age of the independent small farmer, craftsperson, and trader was coming to an end. The population was growing rapidly. A once rural country was becoming dominated by towns and cities. Where there had been one culture, now there were many. Society was becoming complex. City slums, labor strife, and radical political ideas all seemed to be heralding a new, disorderly age associated with immigrants.

Many Americans began to ask: what is an American? What do we want this country to be? Will it be a melting pot or a land of many diverse cultures? Will we keep the door open to people of many lands, or do we now want an America only for "our" kind of Americans?

Hostility to the new immigrants became law in 1924, when Congress legislated strict quotas for the numbers of immigrants from eastern and southern Europe who would be allowed to enter the United States. This body of laws would remain essentially in force until 1965.

The story of the eastern European immigrants is the story about many changes: the changes they brought about in this country; the changes they experienced in moving from the Old World to the new. Their story incorporated major strands of European and American history of the last one hundred years. But it begins long ago, long before there was a United States to come to, in the events that shaped the history and culture of their homelands.

Chapter 1

The Political Landscape of Eastern Europe

> I will suffer, then, as of old; lo, my native tongue and the speech of man will abide in me like a harp with broken strings. But the horrors of the earth are nothing, my anguish for my fatherland is more horrible.[1]
>
> JULIUS SLOWACKI,
> nineteenth-century Polish poet

Some eight and a half million people have emigrated from eastern Europe to the United States since 1850. Who are these people and why did they leave their homes? There are more than twenty nationalities involved in this migration, and it is impossible to trace their histories here. What is possible is to identify peoples and countries and to take an overview of the political conditions in eastern Europe during this era. Most of the countries did not have the same names as they do now. Table 1 (*see*

1

Appendix) identifies the peoples of eastern Europe according to the nations they inhabit today.

Most eastern Europeans are Slavs, an ethnic group thought to have originated in Asia and first settled along the northern slopes of the Carpathian Mountains. From before the Christian era and through the Dark Ages, Slavic tribes migrated westward and settled in different parts of Europe.

The eastern Slavs stayed closest to their place of origin. They are the Russians, Belorussians, and Ukrainians who settled the central and southern Russian plains. Other Slavs headed south to the Balkan Peninsula between the Adriatic and the Black seas. The southern Slavs are Serbs, Croats, Montenegrins, Macedonians, Slovenes, and Bulgars. The western Slavs—Czechs, Slovaks, and Poles— dispersed into the east central plain of Europe.

Other eastern Europeans came of non-Slavic origins. Estonians, related to the Finns, had lived on the shores of the Baltic Sea since ancient times. Latvians and Lithuanians came to the Baltic from farther east, driven by advancing Slavic tribes in the sixth century. On the Black Sea, there was the kingdom of the Dacians, which was conquered by Rome in the second century. Roman soldiers and settlers gave this region the only Latin-based language spoken in eastern Europe. In time, the people of the region came to be called Romanians.

In the ninth century, another non-Slavic people, Magyars, or Hungarians as they are also called, swept into Europe from Asia. They were fierce warriors, and from their main settlement on the Hungarian plain they waged wars of conquest against their neighbors.

Power and territories changed hands many times over the centuries. One century's conqueror would be the next century's conquered. In the thirteenth century, for instance, Bulgaria ruled nearly the whole Balkan Peninsula. In the early fourteenth century, the kingdom of Serbia ruled over Bulgaria.

The conquests that concern this history, however, are those that held into the nineteenth century. For at the time that eastern Europeans were leaving in great numbers for America, most eastern European countries were ruled by foreign powers.

Hungarians were the first to make their conquests stick. Between the tenth and thirteenth centuries, Hungary took its neighbor Slovakia, the province of Transylvania, the kingdom of Croatia, and the West Ukraine. Hungary would control these lands into the twentieth century.

But Hungary itself became the subject of greater empires. The new conquerors were the Ottoman Turks, who originated in central Asia. Earlier Turkish invaders, the Seljuks, had taken most of Asia Minor, or what is now Turkey, from the Byzantine Empire. In the thirteenth century, the Ottomans seized leadership of the Turkish tribes and completed the task. From there, they cut a swath into Europe. The Turks had conquered the Balkan Peninsula by the end of the fourteenth century. In 1526, the Ottomans annihilated the

Hungarian army, killed the Hungarian king Louis, and incorporated most of Hungary into their empire. In 1683, Turkish armies were at the gates of Vienna. They had penetrated almost a thousand miles into Europe. But this was the beginning of their retreat.

Vienna was the capital of Austria. Under the royal house of Hapsburg, Austria had become the leading power in central Europe. Aided by Poland, the Hapsburgs stopped the Turkish advance at Vienna and began a counteroffensive against the invaders. By 1699, the Hapsburg armies had driven the Turks back to the Balkans. On the way, they took control of Hungary's former empire.

Austria now controlled a significant portion of Europe. The relationships among the states involved looked like this:

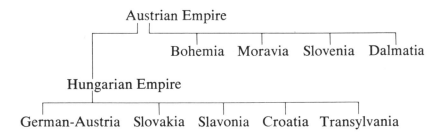

Liberal and nationalist movements in the nineteenth century challenged and began to change Austria's relationship with its subject states. The revolutions that swept Europe in 1848 were a turning point. First, students, workers, and liberals in France took to the streets, then Germans. A large part of Italy was under Austrian rule, and it rose in revolt. So did the people of Hungary, Bohemia, and Austria itself. All the revolutions were eventually put down, and the Hapsburgs reasserted absolute authority over their subjects. But their subjects' yearnings for democratic reform and greater self-government remained.

In 1859, Austria's Italian provinces rose again, and this time succeeded in ousting Hapsburg rule. Meanwhile, Austria's neighbor, the German kingdom of Prussia, was trying to unify the many German states into a German empire, with Prussia at the head. To accomplish this, Prussia had to eliminate the authority Austria still held as the major German state. Prussia declared war on Austria in 1866, and Prussia's victory was so swift that the war was named the Seven Weeks War.

Austria was beset by discontent within and rivalry from without. At this juncture, the Hapsburg emperor decided he had better negotiate some sort of compromise with Hungarian nationalists, who continued to be restless under Hapsburg rule. The result was a revision of the relationship between Austria and Hungary. In 1867 Hungary was elevated to the status of a partner in the empire, although a junior partner. It was given control over most of its internal affairs. Common affairs of the empire, such as foreign relations, defense, and finance, would be regulated by a joint Austro-Hungarian ministry.

The Ottoman and the Austro-Hungarian empires were two of the three great powers which dominated eastern Europe in the nineteenth century. The third, the Russian Empire, appeared last on the scene, but it fast made up for lost time. The destruction of Poland tells most clearly how Russia came into its empire. (A fourth power, Prussia, also played a part in Poland's downfall.)

In the fifteenth and sixteenth centuries, Poland had been the strongest and most prosperous state in eastern Europe. It had been spared both Ottoman and Hapsburg conquest. Russia at the time was just emerging from two centuries of subjugation to Mongol conquerors from Asia.

The Mongols invaded Russia in the thirteenth century, devastating its cities. In the fourteenth century, the kingdom of Lithuania expanded its empire at the expense of its weakened neighbor, annexing Belorussia, the Ukraine, and a part of Great Russia itself. Lithuania and Poland formed a close alliance in 1386, and in 1569 the two kingdoms were formally united. Poland was the dominant power in the Polish-Lithuanian Empire, and at its height, controlled an area stretching from the Baltic down to the Black Sea.

But one thing should be clear by now about the great powers in eastern Europe: they were inevitably challenged by other ambitious states. Three rivals on the Polish borders started to chip away at the Polish dominions. They were Austria, Prussia, and most notably, Russia. As Russia began to rise, Poland began to fall. The Ukraine was their first arena of confrontation.

Polish and Ukrainian serfs were worked hard, and were subject utterly to the will and whim of their masters. The condition of many was hardly distinguishable from outright slavery. A small number of peasants managed to flee their masters to the unsettled areas of the Ukraine. There they formed military communes. These peasant-soldiers were called cossacks, an adaptation of the Turkish word *kazak,* meaning "adventurer."

In 1648, the cossacks rebelled against Polish rule. Their rising grew into a national revolt of the Ukrainian people. But in taking on Poland, they were challenging a mighty state, so the cossacks turned to Russia for military aid. Poland lost the conflict with Russia that followed, but so did the Ukraine. The cossacks had hoped to set up an independent state, but as a result of the Polish-cossack-Russian war, Russia annexed the eastern Ukraine.

In the late eighteenth century, Prussian, Austrian, and Russian designs on Polish territories culminated in three partitions of Poland. Poland had already been weakened by numerous wars and was falling apart under the ineffective rule of its king and nobility. The nation had become an easy and tempting prey. Each of Poland's rivals took sections of the land, and when they were done, nothing of Poland was left.

Russia instigated the first partition by exploiting religious differences in Poland. The Eastern Orthodox churches had separated from the Roman Catholic Church in a series of disagreements spanning the ninth to fifteenth centuries. The central issue was the Orthodox rejection of the authority of the Pope. The Orthodox Church became the established church in Greece, most of the Balkan States, Asia Minor, Russia, and the Ukraine. Russia incited the Orthodox minority in Catholic Poland to appeal to Russia, the most powerful Orthodox nation, to insure their religious liberty. Under Russian pressure, the Polish parliament repealed restrictions against the Orthodox faith, and accepted Russia as spokesman for Orthodox rights. But a faction of Polish nobles bridled at Russian interference in Polish affairs and finally rebelled. In 1772 Russian forces invaded to put down the rebellion.

This state of affairs did not please Prussia and Austria. Were Russia to take all of Poland, then the Russian Empire would extend to the Prussian and Austrian borders. Prussia proposed that each of the three empires take a share of Poland, so that the balance of power in the region would remain unchanged. Not wanting war with Prussia and Austria, Russia agreed.

Russia annexed a portion of Polish Belorussia, to which it had a historical claim. Prussia took West

Prussia from Poland, to which Prussia had an obvious historical claim. Austria took the Polish province of Galicia, to which it had no claim whatsoever, except imperial ambition. In all, Poland lost 28 percent of its territories.

In the twenty years that followed the 1772 partition, the Polish government undertook a series of reforms intended to strengthen the state and solidify the support of the people. In 1791, the Poles codified a new constitution which shifted considerable power from the nobility to the parliament.

Empress Catherine of Russia feared that the new liberal constitution in Poland would inspire liberals in her realm and undermine her autocratic regime. In 1792, Catherine's army invaded Poland, and Prussian forces followed suit. Russia and Prussia were victorious, and in 1793 they divided Poland further between themselves. Only a small section of Poland remained independent, and it lay under the Russian imperial shadow.

In 1794, independent Poland rose up against Russia. The revolt was led by Tadeusz Kosciuszko, a Polish patriot who, seventeen years earlier, had contributed his military services to the Continental army during the American Revolution. Russia smashed the smaller Polish force, and in 1795, with Prussia and Austria, carved up what was left of Poland. Poland disappeared from the map of Europe.

At the beginning of the nineteenth century, then, eastern Europe was parceled out among great empires.

Only two eastern European nations were free of foreign rule. One was Russia, the largest state in eastern Europe. The other was tiny Montenegro, a Balkan province. The Ottomans had tried again and again to take Montenegro, but never succeeded. Montenegro's mountainous terrain and the fierce resistance of its people stymied the Turks time after time. In 1799, the Ottoman Empire finally gave up and acknowledged Montenegro's independence.

The eastern Europeans suffered under all these foreign occupations. The empires had little interest in the welfare of their subjects. Rather, they exploited those subjects for their own gain.

Until the middle of the nineteenth century, most eastern Europeans were peasants, serfs. Serfs were a landlord's property. They worked their lord's fields for him. Sometimes they had to pay the landlord a tax, either in money or in crops. They were not free to leave their estates. But their lords could sell them to other landowners. They were locked into an oppressive system.

In many eastern European countries, foreign nobles had taken the estates as the rewards of conquest. Thus Magyars owned most of the land in Transylvania, and Turks held the land in Serbia and Bulgaria. It didn't matter much to most peasants whether their masters were countrymen or foreigners. Generally, there were only small differences in how they would be treated. Turks regarded their Christian subjects as slaves, but Russian nobles treated their Russian serfs in much the same way.

It mattered much more to the native gentry—the merchants and nobles—that their countries were in foreign hands. Foreign governors kept them from advancing where their skills, ambitions, and class advantages would otherwise have taken them. They were heavily taxed. They were denied political rights. They were degraded to second-class citizenship in their own lands.

It also mattered a great deal to the clergy. Most people were governed by empires that subscribed to different religions from their own. Hungarians—who were two-thirds Catholic and one-third Protestant—penalized the Orthodox Church in Transylvania. Orthodox Russia and Protestant Prussia oppressed the Catholic Church in Poland. Muslim Turks, who regarded all Christians as infidels, elevated the Greeks in their capital, Constantinople, to control of the Orthodox churches in all Turkish lands. In this way, the Ottomans hoped to keep their hands free of Christian affairs. But the Greek clergy oppressed the native clergies and built power bases of their own in the Turkish provinces. Religious discrimination among Christians affected all classes of society. (Jews fell into a special category of religious persecutions. Their situation is considered in chapter 3.) Table 2 (*see* Appendix) shows the established religions of the empires and the subject lands of eastern Europe.

The imperialist philosophy was that weaker nations must serve the will of empires. In 1898, Dr. Satler, a German member of the *Reichstag* (parliament), spelled out to the Reichstag just what this philosophy entailed for Germany's Polish subjects.

> The position between us Germans and you Poles is a natural necessity: it is not the result of ill will or the desire to harm any Polish national, but primarily the consequence of the geographical situation of the territories on which our two nations live. We Germans cannot permit that another nation be the ruler of a territory which is at a distance of only a few hours' ride from the capital. . . . We are compelled to eliminate this nation.

Imperialism meant not only political, religious, and economic domination of subject peoples, it also meant cultural domination, as Dr. Satler went on to aver:

> It is our mutual obligation to seek not only to make loyal citizens of the Prussians of Polish nationality, but also to transform them into real Germans.[2]

The suppression of a national culture might seem minor compared to the enslavement and slaughter that went on under imperialist governments through the centuries. Ten thousand Hungarians were sold in the slave markets of Turkey after the Ottomans conquered their land in 1526. Many thousands of Bulgarians were massacred by Turks in the course of a rebellion against the Ottomans in 1876, a bloodbath that became known throughout Europe as the "Bulgarian Horrors."

But the campaigns to annihilate the native languages and ethnic spirits of subject peoples were another kind of atrocity that the conquered nationalities had to live with every day. German and Russian cultural assaults on the Poles were the most notorious of such programs.

In the Prussian sector of Poland, city and street names were Germanized, and Poles were encouraged to assume German names. The German government took control of Polish schools. Even Catholic schools fell under German Protestant supervision. All instruction was in German.

In 1886, Germany began to buy up the lands of the Polish nobles, who opposed German domination. Germany opened these lands for colonization to German farmers. Over the next twenty-five years, 150,000 Germans moved into Polish lands. Four hundred and fifty German villages sprang up. A new Poland, a German Poland, was being created.

Much the same situation evolved in the Russian sector of Poland. After revolutions in 1830 and 1863, Russia confiscated the lands of the rebels, and only Russians were allowed to buy them. Orphaned boys, and the young sons of rebels, were shipped to Russia to be raised in Russian military schools.

The Russian assault on Polish culture was thorough. Georg Brandes, a Danish historian and literary critic, who visited Poland in 1885, detailed how Russia tried to stamp out the Polish language:

> The Polish language is absolutely forbidden in the University. All lectures, no matter whether delivered by men of Russian or Polish birth, must be in Russian. Not even the history of Polish literature may be taught in the language of the country. Nay, even in the corridors of the University the students are forbidden to speak Polish with each other. . . . So strict is the prohibition . . . that a boy twelve years of age was recently shut up for twenty-four hours in the dark because coming out of school, he said to a comrade in Polish: "Let us go home together."

Brandes tells an even sadder story:

> In a family which I was invited to visit, the following incident happened. The son of the family, a boy of sixteen, the only son of a widow, one evening in the theatre had thrown a wreath to Helena Modrzejewska on behalf of his comrades. A few days later, in obedience to an order from the Minister of Education, the principal of the school called him up, and

told him that he must not only leave the school, but that all future admission to any other school whatever was forbidden him; it was the punishment for having been guilty of a Polish demonstration. The boy went home and put a bullet through his head.[3]

Almost everything that was Polish was forbidden in Poland.

Cultural warfare was waged in almost every subject land, differing only in degree from what was happening in Poland. Hungary tried to "Magyarize" its subject states. Hungarian nobles owned most of the land. Hungarians controlled the church, the police, the courts. Magyar was the official language. The Slovakian, Croatian, and Romanian cultures were denigrated, and the Magyar tradition was glorified. Ironically, Hungarians received similar treatment in turn from Austrian authorities, who tried to "Germanize" them. On the other hand, the Ottoman Empire did not impose their culture on others. The Turks might enslave their subjects, but they did not try to make them accept the Turkish language, religion, and values.

Although Russian peasants were spared cultural and religious attacks, economically they were as downtrodden as any people in eastern Europe. Russian peasants remained serfs until emancipation in 1861. But this did not much improve their lot. The plots of land distributed to the freed serfs by the state were too small to support families adequately.

Peasants had to buy these lands from the state by paying "redemption fees" for a period of forty-nine years, in addition to yearly taxes. As a result, the freed serfs lived in a state of chronic poverty.

Russia was ruled by the most absolute monarch in the world at that time—the Russian emperor, the czar. He shared little of his power with his nobles and ministers, and none with his people. The czarist regime oppressed all classes of Russian society. The czar's secret police spied on student organizations. Writers had to submit books and magazines to censorship before they could be published. Even the Russian Orthodox Church was under state surveillance. The czar's government allowed no outlet for independent political thought.

This was the state of eastern Europe. The mass of people were oppressed by either a foreign government or their own. But in the middle of the nineteenth century, a new political consciousness began to appear and to challenge the order of things.

In Russia, this new consciousness took the form of liberal and radical movements. Liberal thinkers helped bring about the emancipation of the serfs in 1861. New administrative forms of government were needed to replace the authority of the landowners over the peasants. The liberals won their fight to establish district councils, or zemstvos, as local governing agencies. The zemstvos took charge of local services such as health and education. They became the voice of liberal thought, urging progressively greater constitutional reforms. But the czar's reactionary ministers opposed the liberals at every step.

More radical thinkers had to remain underground, where their theories became more extreme. Some were reading the works of Karl Marx, which called for revolution to overthrow the state and the economic stranglehold of the nobles and the rising industrialists. Some radicals formed Socialist and Communist groups. Some became anarchists, opposing all forms of government. Others became Nihilists, trusting no system of values or beliefs whatsoever.

Radical theory led to radical action. Czar Alexander II was assassinated in 1881. The state responded in kind, meeting radical terror with police terror. But revolutionary sentiment nevertheless spread. Many liberals, who had found that they could accomplish little under the czar, became radicals.

In the subject states of Europe, people who had been kept ignorant of their history before the conquerors came, began to discover and take pride in their past. Histories of the Bulgarian and Serbian empires were circulated. Romanians uncovered their supposed Roman ancestry, and published Romanian grammars, for their language was a living link to this heritage. Balkan peoples became aware that their nations had held these lands before the Hungarians and the Turks came.

People who had been forbidden to produce a

native literature began to write. People whose language had been banned from public life began to speak out in their native tongues. They spoke of nationhood, self-determination, independence, and socialism.

The nineteenth century was studded with Nationalist revolutions. In 1863, the Russian sector of Poland rose in rebellion after Russia deliberately changed its military recruitment policy in order to draft members of Polish Nationalist societies. It took Russia two years to eliminate all guerrilla resistance. Thirty thousand Poles died in combat. Fifteen hundred were executed when the rebellion was over.

Nationalist activities were attacked wherever they appeared. One such pocket was the secret students' political club that Louis Adamic and his friend Yanko joined as teen-agers in Austrian-ruled Slovenia before World War I. Adamic regarded his activities in the Yugoslav Nationalist Movement more as an expression of adolescent rebellion and romanticism than as a serious political commitment. But the Austrian government took such activities seriously:

> Soon after Yanko and I got into it, the Yugoslav Movement in Lublyana began to come defiantly and recklessly into the open. In broad daylight, mobs of students dashed through the streets, pulling German signs from

above the entrances to stores and the Austrian double-headed eagle from government buildings, breaking windowpanes, staging small demonstrations. Occasionally a few of them achieved the status of heroes and martyrs within their respective groups by getting their heads bloodied in encounters with the police.

One afternoon fresh from a mass-meeting . . . several hundred youths marched through the streets of the city, singing, shouting, waving the Slovenian colors. They had no permission for the "parade". . . .

"Look!" cried Yanko.

But before I had a chance to turn where he had indicated, a detachment of Austrian cavalry . . . charged the mob from a side street, where it had been waiting for us in ambush. In a moment the soldiers were upon us with drawn sabers.

Then one of the hotheads from our midst hurled a rock at the lieutenant leading the detachment, whereupon that officer commanded:

"Fire!"

. . . We retreated in all directions before the shooting soldiers. Some of the boys sought safety in stores, cafes, and in doorways of private residences.

Suddenly Yanko, who was running ahead of me, dropped. He was dead, a bullet through his head.

. . . Then the firing ceased. The total casualties were two dead and four or five wounded, all of them students. The whole thing happened in less than two minutes.[4]

Nationalism flared most intensely in the Balkans, where it eventually triggered the destruction of the great empires. At first, the main adversary was the Ottoman Empire.

"Turkey is a dying man," Czar Nicholas I had declared in mid-century.[5] The Ottoman Empire was crumbling. Russia had gradually eroded the Turks' hold on the northern and eastern shores of the Black Sea. In the Balkans, Russia allied with Nationalists to hasten the "dying man's" end.

As the most powerful Orthodox state, Russia became the "protector" of the Orthodox living under Ottoman rule. Russia encouraged Nationalist agitation, and began to apply its muscle in the internal affairs of the Ottoman Empire just as it had in Poland.

This concern for the Orthodox had a political reason. The Ottoman Empire controlled the Bosporus and Dardanelles, the straits that led from the Black Sea to the Mediterranean. The Ottomans could block Russian trade and military access from its southern ports. Russia hoped to break this hold and establish Russian influence on the Balkan Peninsula by undermining Turkish rule. This led to three wars between Russia and Turkey in the nineteenth century. By the last of them, in 1878, only

Macedonia and a portion of Bulgaria remained to the Ottoman Empire. Moldavia and Wallachia were united as the kingdom of Romania; Serbia and northern Bulgaria became independent. But all three new states recognized Russia as their protector, which set the stage for new imperial conflicts.

The growing Russian influence in the Balkans alarmed Germany and Austria. So did Balkan nationalism. The combined province of Bosnia-Herzegovina became the focus of nationalist and imperialist struggles.

Bosnia-Herzegovina was occupied by Austro-Hungary. The population was largely Serbian, and the Serbs wished their province to be joined to Serbia. Russia backed this position. Tensions grew even greater as Serbia and Russia also encouraged Croatian nationalists in their quest for liberation from Austro-Hungarian rule.

The Balkan Peninsula was a powder keg, primed for an explosion. It needed just a spark to set it off. That spark was lit on June 28, 1914, in Sarajevo, the capital of Bosnia-Herzegovina.

Archduke Francis Ferdinand, the heir to the Austrian throne, was paying a state visit to the Balkan capital. Gavrilo Princip, a young Bosnian studying in Serbia, crossed back to Sarajevo and shot the archduke and his wife.

As a result of the assassination, Austria sent an ultimatum to Serbia demanding that Austria be given a free hand in suppressing Nationalist and revolutionary societies. In effect, Austria was demanding complete control of Serbia. Serbia would not permit this, nor would Russia. The empires chose sides—Austro-Hungary, Germany, and Turkey on one; Russia, with France and England, on the other. On August 1, Europe plunged into World War I.

All the empires of eastern Europe were destroyed by the war, whatever side they chose. Ottoman Turkey lost its remaining possessions in Europe and the Middle East including Palestine, Germany was defeated and burdened with reparations, the Austro-Hungarian Empire was disassembled. The czarist government was overthrown in the Russian Revolution of 1917, and the Union of Soviet Socialist Republics was born. Other new nations were created from the ashes of World War I: Czechoslovakia (out of Bohemia, Moravia, Slovakia, and Czech Silesia) and Yugoslavia (out of a half-dozen Balkan provinces). Old nations like Poland and an independent Hungary were reborn. The political landscape of eastern Europe was utterly changed.

During this period of political upheaval in eastern Europe eight million people emigrated to the United States. Many were political activists whose lives were in peril if they did not depart. Two and a half million were Jews, who were subjected to special terrors in eastern Europe. But most immigrants were peasants and workers who thought little about politics. Still, peasants had been affected by politics. Cultural oppression demeaned the languages they spoke. Religious persecutions hindered the free exercise of their faiths. Wars and rebellions turned their homelands into battlegrounds.

But before World War I it was the economic consequences of the politics that moved most eastern Europeans to go. The peasants' lot was bad, and things were getting worse. Peasants were heavily taxed to support the imperial states. Their sons were taken to serve in imperial armies. No matter how hard they worked, they would stay poor and oppressed. The Russian czar, the Hapsburg emperor, and the Ottoman sultan were concerned only with power, not with the welfare of the people they ruled.

Chapter 2

Roots: Peasant Life in Eastern Europe

While it is nearly two generations since the old agrarian system based on an unfree peasant class was abolished, its results are by no means a thing of the past. In a Hungarian village which I visited there was an old man who still remembered being beaten as a boy by the landlord's steward for some trivial fault in connection with feudal field work.[1]

EMILY GREENE BALCH

Serfdom vanished late in eastern Europe. The emancipation of serfs occurred in 1848 in the Austro-Hungarian Empire, in 1861 in Russia, and in 1864 in Romania and Russian Poland. This was some 100 years after serfdom ended in France, 500 years after it was phased out in England, and at approximately the same time as slavery ended in the United States—less than 150 years ago.

24

Peasant life was not greatly changed by emancipation. A British physician who settled in Transylvania wrote about the condition of the peasantry ten years before emancipation:

> Among the greatest evils of which the Transylvanian peasant has to complain is the absence of any . . . laws to which he can refer . . . and his almost entire subjection to the will of his master. . . . In some [parts of the country] the landlord takes as much labor as he possibly can extract out of the half-starved creatures who live under him. Here, too, the flogging block is in full vigor; every landlord can order any of his tenants or servants who may displease him [to get] twenty-five lashes on the spot.[2]

And an American historian wrote about conditions he saw in Russia shortly before World War I:

> The *Ispravnik*, or police commissioner, had general supervision over each district. His will was law. He could fine or imprison anyone he chose. . . . He could enter any house at any time of the day or night without a warrant. . . . There was also the *Zemsky Nachalnik*, who had administration of all the rural institutions. . . . He could depose all elected officials of the peasant commune . . . and order any peasant flogged. He belonged to the nobility and naturally would not betray their interests.[3]

The Czech-American historian, Thomas Capek, commented on the peasants of Bohemia:

> For centuries the ruling class drummed into the head of the peasant: obey the Church, obey the government, obey the lords. The archbishop claimed . . . the peasant's soul; the emperor held a . . . mortgage on his body; the lord usurped the fruits of his labor. To the peasant little was left that was free and unencumbered.
>
> Regimented from childhood up to obey and never to command; knowing little or nothing of constitutional liberty, was it any wonder that . . . the old-time Cech [sic] immigrant appeared backward and servile and sheepish?[4]

Empires might change hands. Nationalists might seize power. Serfdom might be abolished. But the hard facts of peasant life remained the same.

And in many respects things grew worse for the peasant class. Emancipation had not been an unqualified boon. In Russia over ninety percent of the taxes collected by the government were paid by the peasant class in some years. Often a peasant's annual rent (for an allotment of land that may have been worked by the same family for generations) and tax obligations would exceed his income. When that happened, he could lose his land.

Many peasants wound up with less land than they had had for their own use before emancipation. These holdings grew smaller as fathers divided up their land among their sons in each generation. In Austrian Galicia, perhaps the poorest province in all eastern Europe, over half the peasant holdings were smaller than five acres; around the turn of the twentieth century, fifty thousand Poles starved each year.

While peasant holdings were shrinking, family size was increasing. Between 1750 and 1850, the population of Europe had nearly doubled, from 140 to 260 million. By World War I, the population was almost 400 million, owing to a sharp decline in infant deaths. No one is sure why this happened. Medical advances of the time were not enough to account for it, and medical services, anyway, were not widely available. But the effect of the population boom was clear: each household had more mouths to feed.

Under these circumstances, there was no way for peasants to improve their state, no matter how hard they worked or how carefully they saved. At best, they could hope to get by. But getting by meant no more than a roof and a few acres of land that a family might hold on to year after year.

A typical farm was a collection of strips of land scattered here and there about the village. This was a result of the old feudal system, whereby the serfs' lands were held communally by the village. The village council or commune assigned strips for cultivation to individual families. Pastures and woodlands were shared by all. A peasant's acres might be scattered over as many as forty different locations.

The village commune also determined how a family farmed. Before World War I, the villages followed a traditional three-field system: one-third of the land for winter crops, such as wheat and rye; one-third for summer crops, barley and potatoes; and one-third lay fallow, or unused, each year, in the belief that this would keep the soil fertile.

Under this system, it was hard for an individual peasant to introduce new or different farming techniques to increase his yield. Many kinds of initiative were stifled. A Polish peasant wrote to his brother in the United States in 1906:

> Summer has been dry this year. . . . It would be well to make a road now to the pasture fields, because it is dry; but in our village people don't unite. Nobody went to make it. I worked alone for some mornings, making the beginning, but I was the only one so stupid; all the others are so clever, and nobody goes to work, although it is difficult to get a better time [for building the road]. Why, laziness and stupidity and darkness will never make anything good.[5]

However, the communal efforts and relationships of the village were a source of support, as well as of frustration. Village communes provided a stable society that continued from generation to generation. Everyone knew everyone, and all knew where they fit in. Everyone had to, and did, pull together, because all depended on each other for their economic survival. The village, with its church and its tavern, was the center of the peasant's social life. The historian Jerome Davis, who lived in Russia for several years before World War I, reported:

> A peasant member of the Duma* once told me of the terrible conditions of his own people, their needs, their wants, their misery, their ignorance. All the same, we have great fun in our village; you ought to come and stay there. There is no such life in the world.[6]

The peasant village was plunked in the middle of the village's fields.

An American historian described a prosperous Czech village in the early twentieth century:

> There is one long street or road, along which are strung the dwelling houses. These are built of brick or stone, covered with plaster, and adjoin one another. . . . The entrance to any of these houses is through a large gate leading into a passageway from which one may enter, at one side, into the dwelling-rooms; on the other, into the stable; and at the rear, to a yard used either as a barnyard or a garden. In the dwelling there are at most four rooms, often only two, and sometimes but one. A huge stove in the corner serves for both heating and cooking purposes. The large shelf over the stove is often used as a sleeping bunk, particularly where

* The Russian parliament which the czar was forced to establish in response to revolutionary demands in 1905.

families are large. . . . Even where there is more
than one room, the kitchen serves as the family
gathering place, dining-room, and bedroom.
"Holy" pictures adorn the walls. The wooden
floors are swept clean. Ample but simple meals
are the rule.[7]

An American traveler described the villages he
saw in Macedonia in the early twentieth century:

Some villages in Macedonia consist of one-
story mud huts, with thatched roofs, devoid of
ceiling, windows, or board floors, one end
serving for the residence, the other for a stable,
with a screen of mud-plastered wattle, slightly
higher than a man's head, between. In the
residence part a fire is made in the middle of
the room, and the smoke finds its way out as
best it may.[8]

A Ukrainian immigrant described the typical
peasant diet in his homeland in the early twentieth
century, which would apply throughout eastern
Europe.

Meat is very seldom used. They live mostly on
vegetables and starchy foods to which they add
salt, pork or lard. Meat is sometimes used on
Sunday or on some holy days. Even if they do
breed cattle, hogs and fowls they cannot use
them for themselves, but must sell them in
order to get money to pay their high taxes and
other necessities. There is no other way to get

money, for there is no industry nor place where they can get it.[9]

Peasants had few animals, and only the well-to-do had horses. Most used an ox or a cow for field work. The poorest peasants dragged their wooden plows behind them across the fields. Harvesting was done by hand, with sickles and scythes.

Mary Boreth, a Hungarian immigrant, describes how produce was taken to market in the early 1900s.

> My mother had to walk many miles carrying the vegetables to the market. Seven miles to the market place, they had to walk. Of course, they had oxen, but they were working in the fields. They used them for the heavy work, and not to drive to the market.[10]

Peasant women worked as hard, if not harder, than the men. Besides cooking, washing, and looking after the children, they milked the cows, fed the chickens, and they worked in the fields alongside the men. Children pitched in, too, as soon as they were able, certainly before the age of ten.

A letter written in 1910 by a Polish woman to her son in the United States conveys the daily toil and cares of a peasant family.

> Dear Son,
> . . . Always these new things, so that my income doesn't suffice. And you know that your father always says: "When anything is not

there, we can do without it." But sometimes it must be had, even if it must be cut out from under the palm of the hand! So, dear son, I beg you very much, if you can, send me a little money. . . . Elzbietka is grown up, Polcia is bigger still, Zonia begins to overtake them, and they all need to be dressed, while it is useless to speak to your father about it. . . . Well, we have nice hogs, nice cattle, and a nice horse, but I must work conscientiously for all this. Your father just excuses himself with his old age, and I may work with the children so that my bones crack. He says: "Then don't keep so much farm-stock, don't work! Do I order you to do all this?" But when he wants anything he has to have it. As to the crops, everything is not bad . . . only we must work so much.

Everywhere only work and work, so that my bones lap over one another. But what can be done? Unfortunately my teeth decline absolutely to work any longer and I must have some new ones put in, but I have not money enough for it, for I have other things to spend it on. So if it is not a great detriment to you I beg you for a few roubles for my teeth. But if not, it cannot be helped. . . .

> Your loving mother,
> ANNA MARKIEWICZ[11]

No matter how hard a family worked, they might still find themselves hard up. Nature could always turn against them. Walery Wroblewski wrote his brothers in America about his worries in the cold spring of 1908:

> We have spring already. All the birds are here —larks, lapwings, storks, swallows, cuckoos, nightingales—in short, all of them. But the spring does not progress favorably. We have St. Stanislaus [day] today, and the trees are still black and don't think of blossoming. Some years ago the orchards had blossomed already at St. Wojciech. Cold wind blows from all sides. I wasted all the food from my barns in feeding my stock; everything is empty. There was no hay. Moreover water flooded the potatoes in early spring . . . and afterwards they froze in the barns. Everything goes on unfavorably.[12]

Periodic droughts and crop failures made life even harder. And when the land failed, people starved. Disease also cut short many lives. Medical care in the rural districts of Russia was almost non-existent, as Jerome Davis observed:

> In America we have one physician to every 800 persons, but in European Russia, in 1912, there was only one for every 13,000 in the cities and towns, and one for every 21,900 in the country.[13]

Educational opportunities for peasants varied from empire to empire. Russia offered the least. Jerome Davis reported:

In 1912, out of a population of one hundred and eighty million, only seven million were in school. Moreover, according to the report of the investigating committee of the third Duma, the educational influence which the schools exerted was insignificant. Many children, soon after leaving, were found to be practically illiterate. The school terms were only for four or five months in the winter, anyway. It is no wonder that at least fifty per cent could not even sign their own names, and nearer seventy per cent could not read.[14]

Elementary schooling was compulsory throughout the Austro-Hungarian Empire by the late 1860s. But, according to Thomas Capek:

The elementary school taught little more than reading, spelling, and arithmetic. The sovereign desired not educated citizens, but loyal and obedient subjects.[15]

The church also often promoted obedience and acceptance of the status quo above spiritual development. This was particularly true of the Russian Orthodox Church, which was, in effect, an arm of the state. Priests praised the peasants' ignorance as holy. They spied on their parishioners for the state police. They spent huge sums of money on gold-leafed altars, and none on social services.

In some of the subject lands of eastern Europe, the Church played a totally different role. In

Romania and Bulgaria, for example, the Church preserved the language and the literature of the people. Priests were leaders of the Nationalist awakenings.

Most peasants did not concern themselves with the politics of their church. They simply believed, and followed the traditions and rites they had learned from their parents. Religion brought them comfort and hope. They looked to God to protect and help them through the hardships. Such expressions as "God be with you," and "Praise the Lord Jesus Christ," were daily salutations between peasants. Whether or not faith was heartfelt, peasants offered daily prayers and attended weekly church services. In the narrow confines of the village, one's religious observances were always under the scrutiny of the neighbors and the village priest.

Louis Adamic, an immigrant from Slovenia, felt that, in his family, religion was as much a matter of custom as of conviction. Adamic recalls his father's practical reasons for urging young Louis to become a priest—which young Louis, in the end, did not do.

> In my father's life . . . religion was of no great moment. He was essentially a practical man who had serious and constant business with the ancient earth. He went to church on Sundays and prayed to God every evening with his family, but I think he did so more because that was the conventional thing to do than

because he felt it necessary. Basically, like most peasants . . . he was a hard realist, a practical man, a fatalist. . . . However, he probably figured, if a son of his was cut out to be a priest —why, well and good. Priests were an important part of the scheme of things. To have a priest in one's family added to one's prestige. . . . He felt that even now peasants in the parish showed him a special sort of deference because his wife's brother was a priest. To have his own son become one . . . would be even better.[16]

Whatever a family's plans for its sons, they could be wrecked by compulsory military service. Marcus Ravage, an immigrant, wrote of the fear of the draft that hung over the heads of young men in Romania early in the twentieth century:

There was the dreadful horror of the recruiting officer constantly lurking in our path like a serpent, ready to spring on a young man just when he had reached the stage where he could be useful to himself and of help to his family. My brother Paul was a case in point. He had struggled for years—ever since he had been twelve—to learn a trade; had served a three-year apprenticeship for his mere bed and board; had then toiled like a slave first for fifty, then for a hundred francs a year. And when at last he had become master of his calling and was about to become independent, along came the scarlet monster and packed him off to its musty barracks, to be fed on black bread and cabbage, to learn senseless tricks with his feet and a gun, to spend days and whole weeks in prison cells, as if he were a criminal, to be slapped in the face like a bad boy, and to live in constant terror of war and the manoeuver for the rest of his life.[17]

In Austria, every man, with a few exceptions, was required to serve three years, and was forbidden to marry until he had completed his service. Poles in the German Empire had to serve four years, under the harsh discipline of Prussian officers. In the Russian Empire, the term was up to six years.

Since families needed income above what their fields provided, many young men took migrant farm work on estates for wages that they would bring home at the end of the season. The working season was long and conditions were hard. In a 1910 letter to their children in America, Jan and Ewa Stelmach of Galicia wrote of their sons who were working in the wheat fields of Prussia:

Our condition is not pleasant, because winter tumbled upon us, snows have been falling since November 22, and it is difficult to go out anywhere. The boys did not come home from Prussia, they wrote that they will come only for Christmas. The cold annoys them, because they must rise at dawn to work and labor long in the evening.[18]

Female children might be sent to work as domestics. Esther Hagler, an immigrant whose family lived in a small lumbering town in the Carpathian Mountains, was sent to work at a very early age.

> There were 12 of us children and each was sent out to earn her keep from age 6 up. I was the eighth of the twelve, and as far back as I can remember I was taking care of other people's children in town for the price of a bowl of soup. At the age of 10 I was considered old enough to work full-time, hence I was sent to a town far from home . . . a place called Riminov. . . . I was expected to scrub hardwood floors, wash clothes, and carry a baby the rest of the time. Of course there were no baby carriages. . . . That was my life for several years.[19]

Sometimes whole families, like Esther Hagler's, would leave the land and settle in towns and cities. They might have lost their fields for nonpayment of taxes and fees. Or perhaps they just gave up. Other times, just the men went to work in trades and factories, sending their wages home. This was often more desirable, because the workers' quarters in the cities were so squalid that the women and children were much better off trying to sustain themselves on the farms.

Working and living conditions in the industrial centers that arose in the late nineteenth century were horrible. In the Baku oil fields in southern Russia, workers lived in barracks built by the oil companies. The historian Miriam Kochan described them:

> These buildings had very few windows and were inadequately ventilated. They were heated by oil stoves which, apart from the fire risk they presented, were dirty, smelly and sooty; and all the buildings were crammed to overflowing with beds made solely from planks. Some companies, where work was done in shifts, provided beds for only half the total number of workers, so that bunks were exchanged as shift relieved shift. In other barracks, married couples lived side by side with single men, sometimes separated by a low curtain, sometimes with nothing at all between them. A report in 1903 told how "the workers, all in greasy, soot-covered rags, covered with a thick layer of grime and dust, swarm like bees in the extremely dirty and congested quarters. A repulsive smell hits you as soon as you try to approach the window."[20]

Conditions were no better in the great cities of Moscow and St. Petersburg. Some workers actually lived with their families in the textile factories where they worked. At night they would sleep on the floor between the machines. Their lives were spent in filth, noise, and darkness. Other workers were housed in cheaply built tenements on the outskirts of the cities. Living quarters were cramped. A family of seven might be renting only half a room, which they shared with another family of seven. The houses were damp and dark, roofs leaked, and the cold Russian winter winds blasted through the holes in the walls. The structures swarmed with roaches and rats.

One can read the distress of the working class in a petition that the workers of St. Petersburg tried to present to Czar Nicholas II on January 22, 1905.

> O Sire, we working men of St. Petersburg, our wives and children, and our parents, . . . have come to you, our ruler, in quest of justice and protection. We are beggars, we are oppressed and overburdened with work; we are insulted, we are not regarded as human beings but are treated as slaves who must suffer their bitter lot in silence. . . .
>
> Our first wish was to discuss our needs with our employers, but this was refused to us: we were told that we have no legal right to discuss our conditions. . . . We asked that wages of casual laborers and women should be raised to one rouble a day, that overtime should be abolished and that more adequate medical attention should be provided for us. . . . We asked that the factories should be rebuilt so that we could work in them without suffering from draughts, rain and snow. . . .
>
> Your Majesty! We are here, many thousands of us; we have the appearance of human beings,

but in fact we have no human rights at all, not even the right to speak, to think, or to meet for discussion . . . for the improvement of our conditions. We are turned into slaves by your officials. Any one of us who dares to raise his voice in defense of the working class is thrown into prison, sent into exile. . . .

Is this, O Sovereign, in accordance with the laws of God, by whose grace you reign? . . . Break down the wall between yourself and your people.[21]

On that January day in 1905—"Bloody Sunday" as it came to be called—two hundred thousand workers of St. Petersburg poured out of the slums and factories. Carrying banners, icons, and portraits of Nicholas, they marched to the Winter Palace, to present their grievances to the czar. Nicholas was not even there; he was at another palace outside the city. But that did not matter, because the marchers never made it to the Winter Palace. The government had been forewarned of the demonstration and had called out troops to deal with it. The workers found their way blocked by soldiers. When they tried to press on, the troops opened fire. The crowd included women and children, and the toll was awful. The government claimed that ninety-two demonstrators were killed, and some three hundred wounded. The actual numbers were probably several times greater.

Bloody Sunday ushered in a year of workers' strikes, military mutinies, and local peasant uprisings—events that were called the Revolution of 1905. It was the precursor of the Revolution of 1917. The czar agreed to some political reforms, but they were few, and they didn't affect the way most peasants and workers lived. They were still poor, still exploited, and still had no say in how their country was run. So it was through all of eastern Europe.

Until the late nineteenth century, the Russian czar and the Hapsburg emperor had been reluctant to lose potential farmers, workers, and soldiers. But now they saw emigration as a way of easing pressures caused by a rapidly growing and dissident population. The peasants demanded more land and lower taxes. The workers wanted unions and the right to vote. The various nationalities wanted self-rule. The liberals wanted democratic constitutions. Socialist, communist, and anarchist revolutionaries wanted to create a new order on the ashes of the old.

Open political agitation and acts of violence against the government spread throughout Russia. The governments resisted change with all their might. Some people gave up hope for improvement in eastern Europe. Some dreaded the long and bloody struggle that seemed to be the only way to bring about change. Many people simply felt that if they couldn't make a decent life for themselves in their homeland, maybe they could somewhere else.

So peasants and workers began to leave for the United States. America presented a dream of opportunity and equality. America was hope.

Chapter 3

Shver Tsu Zayn a Yid (Yiddish Proverb: "It Is Hard To Be a Jew")

> The Crazy Nihilist who hurled a bomb at Czar Alexander II was the ultimate creator of the New York Ghetto and the man who added 3,000,000 Jews to the American population.[1]
>
> BURTON J. HENDRICK

On March 13, 1881, a young revolutionary threw a bomb and killed Czar Alexander II of Russia. The assassin was not Jewish, nor were the other members of the conspiracy. Yet the government responded to the act with its harshest persecutions yet of Russian Jewry.

A Jew in a Russian *shtetl*—the Yiddish name for the rural towns in which more than half of Russia's Jews lived—would have shrugged his shoulders, sighed, and explained with profound fatalism, "*Shver tsu zayn a Yid.*"

It was hard to be a Jew throughout eastern

Europe. For most of Jewish history, it was hard to be a Jew anywhere.

Jews came to Europe after the fall of the ancient kingdoms of Israel and Judah in the Middle East. Through the Middle Ages and beyond, they were the untouchables of Europe's Christian kingdoms. They were forced to live in ghettos, Jewish quarters often enclosed by walls. They were required to wear badges on their clothing identifying them as Jews. They were excluded from trade guilds and forbidden to own land. During the Black Death, a plague in 1347 that carried away about one-third of Europe's population, thousands of Jews were put to death. Scared and superstitious Christians thought that, somehow, Jews had brought the plague upon them.

At some times, in some places, Jews rose high in their adopted lands. In Poland in the sixteenth and seventeenth centuries, they prospered as merchants and as administrators of the nobles' estates. But their success provoked the anger of the oppressed peasants.

As the nobles' agents, Jews collected taxes and feudal dues. They were the visible symbols of the landlords' oppression. Jewish merchants made money in the grain trade, while the serfs who produced the crops hungered. Because the Church said charging interest was evil, Catholics were forbidden to lend money at interest during the Middle Ages. Jews became the principal moneylenders until the seventeenth century. The Church also damned Jews as Christ-killers and heretics. Jew hatred was bred into the Polish populace by economic realities and religious biases.

The peasant hatred of Jews exploded in 1648, during the Ukrainian cossack rebellion against Polish domination. Cossack and peasant armies raged through Poland for the next twenty years. Nobles and Jews were their special targets, as the following letter from a ravaged province reports:

> They slaughtered eight hundred noblemen together with their wives and children as well as seven hundred Jews, also with their wives and children. Some were cut into pieces, others were ordered to dig graves into which Jewish women and children were thrown and buried alive. Jews were given rifles and ordered to kill each other.[2]

One-quarter of Poland's Jewish population died during the cossack wars. Most of the survivors were left in extreme poverty.

Almost 95 percent of the Jewish immigration to the United States in the late nineteenth and early twentieth centuries came from three eastern European states: Austro-Hungary, Romania, and the Russian Empire. In these three lands the discriminations of the Middle Ages continued, and with new and even more vicious twists.

The Austro-Hungarian Empire was the least oppressive. In 1867, its Jews were "emancipated," that is, granted the same rights as other citizens to live and work where they could and to worship as they chose. But centuries of prejudice could not be erased simply by the emperor's signing his name to a proclamation. Jews still encountered prejudice, particularly in Galicia, the Polish province that Austria had seized and that held the empire's largest concentration of Jews.

Business and industry began to develop in Galicia in the late nineteenth century, and a Polish middle class was born. It found itself in competition with Jewish businessmen. In towns and cities, Christians boycotted Jewish merchants, artisans, and manufacturers. At the same time, in the rural areas, Galician peasants were becoming so impoverished that Jews who tramped the back roads as peddlers could no longer depend on much business.

In Romania and Russia, discrimination against Jews was written into law, and the governments tolerated and even promoted violence against Jews.

Romania's Jews were legally classified as foreigners. Since Romania was their home, and they had no other, they were in effect people without a country. They were expelled from the countryside where they had traded with the peasants. They were forced to live in cities and towns, where work and business opportunities for them were almost nil.

Marcus Ravage, who came to the United States in 1900, summarized a Jew's prospects in Romania:

> I reminded my parent of his ambitions for me. . . . Just what did he expect me to turn into? I painted a gloomy picture of our life in

Rumania—the poverty, the absence of every variety of opportunity, the discriminations of the Government against us. Whichever way one turned there were prohibitions and repressions. Supposing I wanted to study law, then "aliens" were not eligible to the bar. The ministry? Rumania forbade the establishment of rabbinical seminaries. . . . When [my father] had engaged in storekeeping in the country and had, by hard toil, succeeded in making a comfortable living, a new law had legislated him and all his kind back into the towns. . . . He was thus doomed to stay forever in the petty business of grain brokerage, which, being the only occupation open to thousands of others, was in a state of such cutthroat competition that even the most competent were hardly able to support their families by it.[3]

Jews were excluded from most jobs and professions. Jewish children were barred from the public elementary school system. Even hospitals would not take in more than a small quota of Jewish patients. The Jews of Romania were outcasts.

Romanian Nationalist feelings ran high long after the country's liberation from the Turks. Non-Romanians were resented; alien influences were blamed for everything that was wrong. Politicians inflamed the populace against Jews, particularly during election campaigns and periodic economic depressions. Officially sanctioned gangs regularly invaded Jewish neighborhoods, looting homes and shops, and assaulting people.

The Jews began to flee. About one-third of Romania's Jewish population emigrated to the United States between 1880 and 1914. The U.S. Secretary of State, John Hay, protested Romania's persecutions in a diplomatic note of 1902. Hay was moved not only by humanitarian feeling but by alarm at the numbers of poor Jews flooding in. Hay charged that Romania was deliberately driving out its Jewish population:

> The condition of a large class of the inhabitants of Roumania has been for many years a source of grave concern to the United States. I refer to the Roumanian Jews. . . . [They] have become reduced to a state of wretched misery. . . . Human beings so circumstanced have virtually no alternative but submissive suffering or flight. . . . [They] are being forced . . . to quit their native country.[4]

In Jewish life in the Russian Empire lie the roots of the majority of America's Jews today. Seventy percent of the Jewish immigrants of the great migration era came from Russian lands. As in Romania, roughly a third of the population took flight, two million coming between 1881 and the start of World War I.

Russia inherited half the Jews of Europe—almost half the Jews in the world—when it took the lands north of the Black Sea from the Turks, and Lithuania, Belorussia, and the lion's share of Poland and the Ukraine, in the late eighteenth and early nineteenth centuries. The czars, suddenly possessed of an unwanted Jewish population, ordered them confined to a "Pale of Settlement"—"pale" meaning an enclosed district. The Pale consisted of the twenty-five provinces newly taken from the Turks and the Poles.

The Russian government tried to quarantine the Jews by keeping them in the Pale. It also tried to force them to convert to Christianity and assimilate with Russians by making their lives as Jews utterly miserable. A conversion scheme devised by Czar Nicholas I illustrates how painfully Jews were made to suffer for their religion. Jews had been barred from the Russian army. But in 1827, Czar Nicholas made them subject to the same twenty-five-year draft as serfs. In addition, from the age of twelve Jews had to serve a preliminary six-year indoctrination term. Boys even younger than twelve were torn from their families to fill the czar's annual quota. They were placed in a hostile military establishment, where they were starved and beaten until they accepted the Eastern Orthodox faith. Draftees would either convert or die. Their families would never see them again. When a boy was taken, his parents said the Jewish prayer for the dead.

Alexander Herzen, a Russian writer and revolutionary, described coming upon a convoy of Jewish inductees in Siberia, where he was in exile for his political activities:

". . . They die like flies," [the officer in charge told me]. "You see, these little Yids . . . aren't used to sloshing around in the muck for ten hours at a time without anything to eat except bread. . . ."

The children were gathered and organized into columns. It was one of the most horrible sights I've ever seen. . . . The boys of twelve or thirteen were still in fair condition, but the eight- and ten-year-olds! . . . Pale, bruised, fear-ridden, there they were, in their military greatcoats, with their stand-up collars, gazing with both supplicating and resigned looks at the soldiers who pushed them around while lining them up. Pale lips, dark rings around their eyes, which reflected either fever or cold. And these poor children, without care, without love, exposed to the biting Arctic winds, were on their way to the grave.[5]

Nicholas's son, Alexander II, reformed the conscription laws in 1874. The term of active service for all conscripts was reduced to six years, and the special preliminary term for Jews was abolished. Alexander, the "Liberator Czar" who had freed Russia's serfs, also allowed certain privileged classes of Jews to live outside the Pale: merchants whose business activities were considered to be in the empire's interests; artisans and professionals who could provide needed services in other areas. Most Jews were confined to the Pale, however.

The language of daily life in the Pale was Yiddish. Jews had brought this medieval German dialect eastward with them when they had been driven from Germany by superstitious peasants and clergy in the years of the Black Death. Smatterings of Polish and Russian sprinkled in over time, along with touches of Hebrew, the Jewish language of prayer. All the Jews of eastern Europe spoke Yiddish, whatever their country.

Sholom Aleichem, the most popular Yiddish writer, grew up in a *shtetl* in Belorussia, or White Russia. In his stories, Sholom Aleichem transformed his town into the fictional Kasrielevky. Maurice Samuel, a folklorist, described Kasrielevky as a typical *shtetl* of the 1860s and '70s:

> Kasrielevky is also Kozodoievka and Bohopolie and Bohslav and any one of a hundred Jewish or half-Jewish centres in old White Russia. The town itself is a jumble of wooden houses clustering higgledy-piggledy about a market-place at the foot of a hill. All around is the spaciousness of mighty Russia, but Kasrielevky is as crowded as a slum, is in fact a slum. . . .
>
> The streets of Kasrielevky—let us be courteous and call them that— are as tortuous as a Talmudic* argument. They are bent into question marks and folded into parentheses.

* Referring to the Talmud, or books of Jewish law. Talmudic scholars were known for their elaborate and intricate arguments about the meaning of each point of law.

They turn back upon themselves absent-mindedly, they interrupt themselves. . . . They run into [dead ends]. . . . Sewerage and paving are as unknown in Kasrielevky as the steam train. . . .

At the heart . . . is the market-place, with its shops, booths, tables, stands, butchers' blocks. Hither come daily, except during the winter, the peasants and peasant women from many miles around, bringing their live-stock and vegetables, their fish and hides, their wagonloads of grain, melons, parsley, radishes, and garlic. They buy, in exchange, the city produce which the Jews import, dry goods, hats, shoes, boots, lamps, oil, spades, mattocks, and shirts. The tumult of the market-place of Kasrielevky is one of the wonders of the world. . . . For besides the lusty haggling in Russian-Yiddish and Yiddish-Russian, there is the bleating of goats, the braying of donkeys, the neighing of horses, the clucking of hens, and on top of it all, persistent and piercing, the chorus of children's voices from the *cheders,* the one-room Hebrew schools, which are gathered about the market-place. Here, too, the Kasrielevkites have built their synagogues, prayer-houses . . . where services are . . . noisy, hearty, enthusiastic, and even slightly riotous.

But despite all the commerce in the marketplace, Kasrielevky was a town of poor people.

The [proper] merchants . . . could be counted
on [one's] fingers and toes. . . . Most of the
market-place was occupied by pedlars,
hangers-on, . . . women with a basket of eggs
or a bundle of old clothes. . . . Rich or poor,
pedlars or artisans, their livelihood was drawn
from the market-place, and from the semi-
annual fairs. It depends, naturally, on what
you call a living. . . . Yerechmiel Moses, the
Hebrew teacher [a character in Shalom
Aleichem's stories], blind in one eye and short-
sighted in the other, used to wear spectacles
without lenses. Asked why, he would answer
triumphantly: "Well, it's better than nothing,
isn't it?"[6]

Condemned to a never-ending scrambling to make
their livings, and faced with the vast hostility of
Russia around them, Jews developed an ironic
humor about their condition. It was a way of re-
lieving the pain with laughter. It was a way, also,
of holding on to their sanity under persecution.

Although some towns were 75 percent or more
Jewish, Jews accounted for only about 12 percent
of the Pale's total population. They lived amid
Russian, Ukrainian, and Polish peasants and townspeople. Their Christian neighbors provided the Jews
with their livelihood, for Jews continued in their
traditional functions of shopkeepers and trades-
people. But the Christians also presented a constant
threat. Since they bought from Jews, and borrowed

money from Jews, it was easy for them to think that Jews were exploiting them, particularly when times were hard. As the nineteenth century progressed, there were recurring outbursts of Christian rage, until the Pale began to run with Jewish blood.

The assassination of Czar Alexander II was the turning point. The next czar, Alexander III, cracked down on revolutionaries, liberals, on anyone who dared be critical of the state. He was particularly suspicious of the non-Russian people in his empire. Alexander's harsh new order called for the suppression of Polish culture and the destruction of Russian Jewry. Konstantin Pobedonostsev, the minister of religion, set forth the czar's goals: "A third of the Jews will convert, a third will die of hunger, and a third will emigrate."[7] The last is what happened.

There were new discriminatory laws. The hated May Laws, issued in May 1882, limited the movements and opportunities of Jews more than ever. Jews were expelled from most of the villages. Since so many depended on business with the peasants for their livelihood, they were sentenced to destitution. They had no choice but to live in cities, where the Jewish quarters were soon overflowing.

In the next ten years, permits for Jews living outside the Pale were revoked in one region after another. Families were uprooted, and whatever gains they had made wiped out. They rejoined the pauperized throng in the Pale. The most brutal of these evictions took place in Moscow. To "purify the sacred historic capital,"[8] the czar ordered twenty thousand Jews to leave on the Jewish holiday of Passover, in 1891. Police rounded up the Jewish population, and marched them in chains to the railway station.

The Jewish quarters of the Pale became vast poorhouses. An American visitor recorded his impressions of the town of Berdichev in the province of Kiev in 1891:

> It was . . . an overcrowded place, made up for the most part of old and unsanitary rookeries, in which was huddled one of the poorest populations to be found anywhere in Europe. By August, 1891, it was said that fully twenty thousand additional Hebrews had been driven in from the surrounding countryside. The spectacle of their poverty and squalor was something too sickening for words. The whole place, with its filthy streets, its reeking half-cellars under the overhanging balconies, and its swarming throngs of unwashed, unkempt wretches, packed into the narrow thoroughfares on the lookout for food, made a picture scarcely human.[9]

The Russian governor of Bessarabia wrote:

> The houses along second-rate . . . streets are occupied in unbroken succession by stores, big and small, shops of watch-makers, shoemakers, locksmiths, tinsmiths, tailors, carpenters, and so on. All these workers are huddled together

in nooks and lanes amidst shocking poverty. They toil hard for a living so scanty that a rusty herring and a slice of onion is considered the tip-top of luxury and prosperity. There are scores of watch-makers in small towns where the townsfolk, as a rule, have no watches. It is hard to understand where these artisans . . . get their orders and patrons.[10]

Golda Meir, who was prime minister of Israel from 1969 to 1974, first came to the United States as a child of eight in 1906. In her memoirs, Meir recalled her early years in Kiev:

There was never enough of anything, not food, not warm clothing, not heat at home. Even now, from that very distant past, I can summon up . . . the picture of myself sitting in tears in the kitchen, watching my mother feed some of the gruel that rightfully belonged to me to my younger sister, Zipke. Gruel was a great luxury in our home in those days, and I bitterly resented having to share any of it, even with the baby. . . . I am glad that no one told me then that my older sister, Sheyna, often fainted from hunger in school.[11]

Beyond the daily horrors of poverty were the periodic terrors of pogroms. These organized rampages through Jewish communities, during which homes were sacked and people beaten and killed, were the second phase of the campaigns of Czar

Alexander III, and his son, Nicholas II, against Russia's Jews. The first large wave of pogroms swept the Pale after the murder of Alexander II. Government officials and government-backed newspapers spread rumors that Jews killed the czar. Police and soldiers stood by as mobs looted, burned, raped, and killed. Nearly one hundred Jews were killed or maimed, and thousands of homes and shops were destroyed in the pogroms of 1881 and 1882.

The most infamous pogrom erupted during the reign of Nicholas II, the last czar, on Easter morning, 1903, in Kishinev, the capital of Bessarabia. A Christian boy had been found killed, his body mutilated. Although the boy's uncle admitted the crime, the Bessarabian newspaper charged the Jews of Kishinev with ritual murder. This was a revival of the medieval myth that Jews required the blood of Christians to prepare matzos, the ceremonial bread that they ate on their holiday, Passover. Handbills circulated throughout Kishinev, urging the Jews to be punished. A Russian newspaper correspondent reported:

> During the two days of Easter, an enraged crowd of Christians, made up of both young people and adults, of workers and even of men in uniform, and of civil servants, pillaged and destroyed all of the Jewish houses, their shops and their stores, and killed and wounded many people, among them a great number of women and children. The assassins simply threw the

latter from heights of two or three stories onto
the pavement below. Several synagogues have
been looted, and the rolls of the Torah* torn
and defiled. In some synagogues when the
beadles tried to resist the attackers, they were
beaten into senselessness. All the streets are
covered with a thick layer of feathers and down
from torn quilts, and often the furniture of the
looted houses has been broken into bits and
pieces. Even the flooring, the stoves and the
walls have not been spared, but have been
destroyed as well. I was witness in 1882 to the
looting in Kiev, but what I saw there is nothing
compared to my observations here during these
two days.[12]

Pogroms became a fact of Jewish life. The religion
that so provoked other people was for the Jews
their greatest treasure. Ida Richter, who emigrated
to the United States in 1907, recalled:

My family was very orthodox. We couldn't
wait for the Sabbath day, so we used to dress
up Friday, wash our hair and put on a clean
dress; and the house was cleaned, the *challeh*†
was baked, the table set, make the beds, and
the chores for the next day was ready. And
those little Gentile children used to go to the

*The Old Testament, the Jewish Bible, which is written
on scrolls and kept at the altars of the synagogues.
† A ceremonial braided bread eaten on the Sabbath.

government school. I used to be so sorry for
them, they haven't got a Sabbath like me.[13]

In the late nineteenth century, two nonreligious
ideologies captured the imaginations of Russia's
Jews—particularly the younger generation. They
were Zionism and socialism. Zionism taught that
Jews would never be safe till they had a country of
their own. Socialism held that workers of all religions and nationalities must unite against their common oppressors—capitalists, landowners, and the
state.

Religion had helped Jews accept and endure injustice. The new ideologies moved them to protest
injustice. Jews began to think about escape from
the enclosed world of the Pale, and the passions of
many turned from prayer to action.

Some threw themselves into efforts to establish
Jewish colonies in Palestine, a part of the Ottoman
Empire. Others joined socialist parties, organized
labor strikes, and spread revolutionary doctrine.
Needless to say, the czar did not welcome either of
these developments. Zionism meant disloyalty to
Russia. Socialism was a challenge to the state. Golda
Meir recalled the dangers that Zionists and socialists
ran:

> At fourteen, [my sister] Sheyna was a revolu-
> tionary, an earnest, dedicated member of the
> Socialist-Zionist movement, and as such doubly
> dangerous in the eyes of police and liable to
> punishment. Not only were she and her friends

"conspiring" to overthrow the all-powerful czar, but they also proclaimed their dream to bring into existence a Jewish socialist state in Palestine. In the Russia of the early twentieth century, even a fourteen- or fifteen-year-old schoolgirl who held such views would be arrested for subversive activity, and I still remember hearing the screams of young men and women being brutally beaten in the police station around the corner from where we lived.[14]

At the same time eastern Europe was buzzing with the opportunities and liberties America offered.

In the end, it is not surprising that so many Jews fled eastern Europe. More surprising is the number who stayed. Eastern European Jews lived always on the brink of new atrocities. In 1882, the year that he left Russia for the United States, George Price wrote in his diary:

> Am I not despised? Am I not urged to leave? Do I not hear the word *zhid** constantly? Can I even think that someone considers me a human being capable of thinking and feeling like others? Do I not rise daily with the fear lest the hungry mob attack me? . . . It is impossible . . . that a Jew should regret leaving Russia.[15]

* A derogatory Russian word for "Jew."

Chapter 4

The Taste of America

"America" was in everybody's mouth. Business men talked of it over their accounts; the market women made up their quarrels that they might discuss it from stall to stall; people who had relatives in the famous land went around reading their letters for the enlightenment of less fortunate folks; . . . children played at emigrating; old folks shook their sage heads over the evening fire, and prophesied no good for those who braved the terrors of the sea . . . all talked of it, but scarcely anybody knew one true fact about this magic land.[1]

MARY ANTIN

Immigrants are people reacting to forces that are pushing them out of their homeland, and forces that are pulling them toward a new land.

In eastern Europe, the "push" consisted of religious and cultural persecutions, political tyranny,

61

and economic hardships. Many eastern Europeans came to feel that they could never achieve the kind of life they wanted in the lands where they had been born.

The "pull" of America was the message of the Declaration of Independence: "We hold these truths to be self-evident, that all men are created equal. . . ." It was the attraction of a young land that was growing, that needed hands to farm, build, and produce. It was the dream of better wages, better opportunities, a better life.

Eastern Europeans were among the last Europeans to respond to the lure of America. Most of them—the peasants—couldn't even think of leaving before the middle of the nineteenth century. They were tied to serfdom. They had little or no information about life outside their own villages, much less overseas.

There were, though, occasional individuals and small groups from eastern Europe drawn to America from earliest Colonial times. They were from the higher ranks of society—artisans, merchants, soldiers, nobles. Some came for the adventure of building a new society and to make their fortunes. Six Poles arrived in Jamestown, Virginia, in 1608, just a year after the colony was founded. Among them were glassblowers and tarmakers who used their skills to establish the colony's first industries. Polish teachers founded the first Latin school in New Amsterdam. Czech merchants set up business in the Dutch colony.

Some immigrants were attracted by the promise of religious and political liberties. Seven hundred Czech Protestants settled in Pennsylvania between 1741 and 1762. There they found the religious freedom that Catholic Austria had denied them in Bohemia and Moravia. Their settlements of Bethlehem, Nazareth, and Lititz are still centers of the Moravian faith today.

Hungarian and Polish officers answered the call of the American Revolution and enrolled in the Continental army. Many were political exiles who had defended, unsuccessfully, their own countries' freedoms against the aggression of the European empires. They were drawn by the chance to win glory and to strike a blow for liberty against another European empire.

Most outstanding among these were two Poles. Count Casimir Pulaski transformed the ragtaggle American cavalry into an effective fighting force. He was killed during the siege of Savannah in 1779. His compatriot, Tadeusz Kosciuszko, a brilliant military engineer, designed the American fortifications at Ticonderoga, Saratoga, and West Point. Kosciuszko distinguished himself again as a friend of liberty some twenty years after the Revolutionary War. He had returned to Poland, led the ill fated 1794 rising against Russia, and come back to the United States once more, after two years in a Russian prison. Leaving the United States for Europe for the last time in 1798, he drew up this will:

I, Tadeusz Kosciuszko . . . hereby authorize
my friend Thomas Jefferson to employ the
whole [of my property] in purchasing Negroes
from among his own or any other and giving
them liberty in my name.[2]

A Polish Jew, Haym Salomon, had been a wealthy
merchant in Poland. A patriot, he'd had to flee for
his life after the first partition. He quickly became
an American patriot and worked his European
banking connections to raise money to arm and feed
the Continental army.

After each unsuccessful uprising in eastern
Europe, political exiles made their way to the
United States. Polish activists arrived after revolu-
tions in 1830, 1849, and 1863; Hungarian and
Czech leaders came after the 1848 revolutions.

In the mid-nineteenth century, the promise of
gold and land began to lure independent farmers
and workers. News of the gold strike in California
created a great stir in Bohemia and Croatia. Articles
like the following appeared in the Czech press in
1849:

Reports continue to arrive from California con-
cerning large quantities of gold unearthed
there. Nuggets of gold ore weighing as much as
a pound, in some cases two, have been found.
There are instances on record of emigrants
making in gold digging and in trading with the
Indians as much as $30,000. The average earn-

ings of a person per day amount to $100. . . .
A merchant's clerk commands $3,000 a year.[3]

Reports like this helped shape the popular impression that in America the streets were "paved with gold."

Croatians embarked on what was a three-month sailing journey, down the Adriatic Sea, across the Mediterranean and the Atlantic, and around Cape Horn to the Pacific and the California coast. Czech immigrants usually landed in eastern ports. From there they made their way cross-country by rail, boat, and covered wagon. Many never saw the gold fields. They were sidetracked by the attractions of the rich lands they were passing through. Czech settlements sprang up in the farmlands of Wisconsin, Minnesota, Iowa, and Texas, and in a dynamic young trading center, Chicago.

Word began to spread through eastern Europe about the opportunities and liberties to be found in the United States. Shipping companies placed newspaper ads to entice immigrant passengers. Many American states issued pamphlets promoting themselves to new settlers.

Come! In Wisconsin all men are free and equal before the law. . . . Religious freedom is absolute. . . . No religious qualification is necessary for office or to constitute a voter; all that is required is for the man to be 21 years old and to have lived in the state one year.[4]

Minnesota advertised the opportunity to own good land.

> To Laboring Men, who earn a livelihood by honest toil; to Landless Men, who aspire to the dignity and independence which comes from possession in God's free earth; to All Men of moderate means, and men of wealth, who will accept homes in a beautiful and prosperous country. . . . It is well to exchange the tyrannies and thankless toil of the old world for the freedom and independence of the new . . . it is well for the hand of labour to bring forth the rich treasures hid in the bosom of the NEW EARTH.[5]

Word went out, too, from the early arrivals in America. Father Moczygemba, a Franciscan monk, visited Texas in 1851 and returned home to convince an entire Polish village to follow him back. In 1854, eight hundred men, women, and children landed at a Texas gulf port. Carrying the large cross from the steeple of their village church in Silesia, Father Moczygemba led them off the ship. The immigrants trekked inland to found near San Antonio the first Polish settlement in the United States. They named it Panna Maria, in honor of the Virgin Mary. A Texan wrote:

> The arrival of the colony was one of the most picturesque scenes in my boyhood. . . . Up to that time, the people of Texas were entirely English speaking but for a few colonies from

Germany. . . . Simple frontier people like ourselves have never seen anything like the crowd
which passed along the road that day. There
were some eight or nine hundred of them. They
wore the costumes of the old country. Many of
the women had what, at that time, was regarded as very short skirts, showing their limbs
two or three inches above the ankle. Some had
on wooden shoes and, almost without excep-
tion, [the men] all wore broad-brimmed, low-
crowned black felt hats, nothing like the hats
that were worn in Texas.[6]

Ultimately it was not land that lured the millions
from eastern Europe, but America's growing industries. During the half century after their emancipation, eastern Europeans were discovering how hard
it was to manage as independent peasants and
laborers in their backward and exploitative econo-
mies. As education became more available and
communications improved, they started to read
about life outside their villages and cities, and outside their countries. New railroads connected inland
regions to the seaports. New steamships made ocean
voyages more tolerable and less expensive than they
had been by sail. At the same time that eastern
Europeans were experiencing the "push" of worsen-
ing conditions, they were also finding it more
feasible to go. A Ruthenian priest in Galicia told
the following story of "the first man who went to
America" from his province:

The peasants cannot live on their land. It has been subdivided and subdivided until a man has too little to get a living by, even as they live here. In some places they eked it out by weaving cloth on old house looms during the winter, and hawking it about in the summer. Then the railroad was put through. . . . That was about 1875. This road brought in factory products from Silesia and other places, and ruined weaving and all the old home industries. One of these weavers, a Pole from about Jaslo I think, used to come up this way with his goods. . . . The last time he came was a few years after the railroad was built, and he said his trade was ruined, and he was thinking of going to America. He had heard [in his travels] across the mountains in Hungary that people were going to the United States, and doing well there.[7]

It was the new age of the factory, the steel mill, the coal mine, the railroad. Great numbers of workers were needed to run the machines, pour the metal, dig the ore, lay the rails. America looked to Europe for labor, advertising jobs where earlier it had advertised land.

Many of the immigrants came intending to stay only a few years. They planned to work hard, save their money, and return home to buy enough land to support themselves and their families. In some years, the number of eastern Europeans leaving the

United States to return home equaled half the number of those coming into the country.

"Birds of Passage" they were called, the immigrants who stayed in America just a few years. But many didn't return home at all: some because they hadn't the money and saved the fortunes they thought they would; some because they got used to life in the United States and found it hard to backtrack. The men sent money home to pay for the women to join them. They began to raise families, and put down roots in new American ethnic communities.

Jews were the only eastern European group who, as a whole, set out from their homes knowing they were going once and for all. Russia, Galicia, and Romania offered them nothing to come back to. If the menfolk first made the journey, they sent for the women and children as soon as they were able. Many families set out together.

By sending money home, either to help their relatives there or bring them to America, the earlier immigrants created the impression that they had found prosperity in the new country. "Birds of Passage" returning home described towering cities and throbbing industrial centers that fired the imaginations of those who had not yet come. Immigrants tended to cast their American experiences in the best possible light, exaggerating or inventing achievements to impress the folks back home or to keep them from worrying. So the news they sent back told more stories of success than of failure.

A U.S. Immigration Commission on Slavic Immigration reported in 1907:

> In the large majority of cases . . . the immediate inducement to emigrants to leave home and sail for America comes in the form of personal letters from friends or members of their own families already in the United States.[8]

A letter from a young Polish immigrant, working as a scrubwoman in a Chicago hotel in 1912, painted a rosy picture of how she was getting on:

> I am getting along well, very well. I have worked in a factory and I am now working in a hotel. I receive 18 (in our money 32) dollars a month, and that is very good. . . . We eat here every day what we get only for Easter in our country. We are bringing over Helena and brother now. I had $120 and I sent back $90.[9]

Mary Antin's father, a Russian immigrant writing in the early 1890s to the family that would soon follow him to Massachusetts, praised the United States as a land of social equality:

> In America it was no disgrace to work at a trade. Workmen and capitalists were equal. . . . The cobbler and the teacher had the same title, "Mister." And the children, boys and girls, Jews and Gentiles, went to school! Education would be ours for the asking, and economic independence, also, as soon as we were prepared.[10]

When Mary Antin herself arrived, young and enthusiastic, she wrote back to her friends in Russia:

> In the beginning my admiration was spent on
> . . . the splendors of America: such as fine
> houses, gay shops, electric engines and apparatus, public buildings, illuminations, parades.
> My early letters to my Russian friends were
> filled with boastful descriptions of these glories
> of my new country. No native citizen of
> Chelsea [Massachusetts] took such pride and
> delight in its institutions as I did.[11]

These letters created a stir in the old villages and neighborhoods. And if an immigrant sent back money along with the good news, it seemed proof that all the wonderful tales were true. A Bulgarian immigrant, Stoyan Christowe, recalled a money order that a villager received from a relative in the United States:

> It was that magic slip of paper, more than the
> wonders which the letter narrated, that started
> the exodus to America and changed the life of
> Selo and the neighboring villages. That piece
> of paper from America robbed Selo of the
> tranquility which it had enjoyed for decades.
> All at once people began borrowing left and
> right. They mortgaged vineyards, meadows,
> houses, to the merchants in the town, for
> enough money to pay their passage to the incredible land.[12]

Louis Adamic recalled:

> As a boy of nine, and even younger, . . . I experienced a thrill every time one of the men of the little community returned from America. Five or six years before, as I heard people tell, the man had quietly left the village for the United States, a poor peasant clad in homespun, with a mustache under his nose and a bundle on his back; now, a clean-shaven *Amerikanec*, he sported a blue-serge suit, buttoned shoes . . . a black derby, a shiny celluloid collar, and a loud necktie made even louder by a dazzling horseshoe pin, which rumor had it, was made of gold, while his two suitcases of imitation leather, tied with straps, bulged with gifts from America for his relatives and friends in the village. In nine cases out of ten, he had left in economic desperation, on money borrowed from some relative in the United States; now there was talk in the village that he was worth anywhere from one to three thousand American dollars.

The returnees boasted of their accomplishments, and described sharp contrasts between life in Slovenia, and the life to be had in America:

> In America one could make pots of money in a short time, . . . wear a white collar, and have polish on one's boots like a *gospod*—one of the gentry—and eat white bread, soup, and meat

on weekdays as well as on Sundays, even if one were but an ordinary workman to begin with. In Blato no one ate white bread or soup and meat, except on Sundays and holidays, and very few then.

In America one did not have to remain an ordinary workman. There, it seemed, one man was as good as the next. There were dozens, perhaps scores, or even hundreds of immigrants in the United States, one-time peasants and workers from the Balkans—from Carniola, Styria, Carinthia, Croatia, Banat, Dalmatia, Bosnia, Montenegro, and Serbia—and from Poland, Slovakia, Bohemia, and elsewhere, who, in two or three years, had earned and saved enough money working in the Pennsylvania, Ohio, or Illinois coal-mines or steel-mills to go to regions called Minnesota, Wisconsin, and Nebraska, and there buy sections of land each of which was larger than the whole area owned by the peasants in Blato. . . . Oh, America was immense—*immense!*[13]

In truth, however, most immigrants had rough going all their lives in the United States. They worked at backbreaking jobs for low wages. They lived in slums. They were confused by a different language and strange ways. They were cheated, exploited, and suffered discrimination. Here are excerpts from letters that went back to Poland telling the bad news:

Dear Parents, always it will be better for you to live here than there . . . if you're to break your back on some master's land, do it here on your own.

If you complain so much about your miseries, sell everything and come to America with the children, because it isn't the work here that's so bad, but the loneliness. . . . I'm always a stranger among strangers here.

Here they pick out their workmen like cattle at the market, but you can make a life for yourself better than the landed gentleman at home.

In winter, it is very hard when the factories stop. . . . In winter you can make so many debts that it will take you all summer to get out of them. . . . So don't come here right now, because two thousand souls join us every week and the work is scarce.

This is no Golden Land, but it is a new land; here you break your back for 12 hours a day, and back home they're thinking that they'll be filling their aprons with gold the minute they've come. . . . In America you will spill more sweat in one day than in a week back home. . . . But I will not go back if someone was to give me the master's estate. . . . Once you have tasted America, there is no way to go back to those old miseries.[14]

Chapter 5

Departure and Arrival

For the first time in my life I saw a railroad station, travelled on a train, passed through large towns and cities, and, finally, I travelled on a huge ship over the vast ocean to New York.[1]

JAMES D. BRATUSH

Going to America was a great adventure. The journey always began with leave-taking, a difficult, emotion-filled episode. Marcus Ravage recalled:

> My mother set about with a heavy heart to prepare for the great day which I looked forward to so impatiently and which she so horribly dreaded. For the next four weeks she knitted socks, and made me underwear of flannelette, and sewed buttons, and mended my shirts and my old overcoat. . . . She filled

several jars with jam for me and one or two with some of her far-famed pickles. . . . "You will write us, dear?" she kept asking continually. "You won't forget your old father and mother when the Lord blesses you with riches. You won't forget, will you? Promise me again, my son. . . ."

Just before train-time she put the gold-clasped prayerbook into my grip which my father had given her on their betrothal and sewed two gold napoleons into the lining of my waistcoat. She seemed calm and resigned. But when the train drew into the station she lost control of her feelings. As she embraced me for the last time her sobs became violent and father had to separate us. There was a despair in her way of clinging to me which I could not then understand. I understand it now. I never saw her again.[2]

The first leg of the journey from eastern Europe was to the seaports on the coast: Riga, Danzig, and Hamburg on the Baltic Sea; Bremen, Rotterdam, and Antwerp on the North Sea; Cherbourg on the English Channel. The first hurdles on the journey were the border crossings into western Europe.

Some immigrants left their countries illegally, without proper passports. Often they were young men evading the draft or political activists escaping the police. Since the male head of the family was the one who had to sign for passports, Nina Goodenov and her mother could not get passports to leave the Ukraine in 1911 because Nina's father refused to let them go. Without proper papers their trip was a nightmare:

When you left the country illegally there were people who tried to make a dollar out of you. They called themselves agents and promised to take care of crossing the border. That was the most difficult thing—crossing the Russian border to a different country. For us it was Austria. This crossing I will never forget.

We went to a little village. We were hidden in a peasant's house for a while. Then the agents put all our baggage onto a wagon and at midnight, they said, "It's time to go." They put us in that wagon, too. But climbing over the baggage, my mother fell off, and hurt her back very badly. . . .

We finally reached some water that we had to cross. We had to be careful that no one should hear us—the border guards—or we would be shot. I was no problem—the agent just took me in his arms and crossed me over to the other side, and told me to shut up, not utter a sound. But it was different with my mother. The agent didn't even have a boat; he had what you call a raft, which he steered with one oar. And my mother had a hurt back. She fell into the water trying to get onto the raft. That's all I saw because I passed out.

As the journey continued, Nina learned that she would get no help unless she could pay for it:

When I came to I was in a house where they kept all the immigrants. Everybody was there except my mother and our baggage. I was just sitting there, crying my heart out: "Where is my mother?" And I was terribly hungry. I asked the agent to give me something to eat, and he asked me if I had any money. I said "No," and he said, "Can't eat. We don't give food for nothing."

And so I just sat like that all day long, crying, until one of the peasants brought in my mother in wet clothes, and some of our baggage. The rest of it was stolen.

My mother must have had a fever of about 104°. I asked, "Why didn't you take off your wet clothes?" She said, "I was afraid because I had a little money inside my blouse and that would have been taken away from me." Anyway, she became very ill. We were supposed to go to Germany. But she couldn't move, so we had to stay in that house in Austria.

We were there about ten days, and my mother was very, very sick, and terribly uncomfortable. I had to sleep on the floor and she slept on a cot. The people where we stayed were so mean. When I asked for a pail of water to put some cold compresses on her head, I had to pay for it. . . .

After ten days we were able to leave, and we came to Hamburg where a boat to America was waiting for us.[3]

Thirteen-year-old Stoyan Christowe, who left Bulgaria with four men from his village, had an easier time.

Agents from the steamship company met us at all cities where we changed trains and remained with us until we were safely put on the next train. Sometimes the agents rode with us great distances and did not turn back until they delivered us into the care of other representatives of the line. They pinned red buttons with white stars [for the White Star Steamship Line] on our coat lapels so that it was easy for the agents to pick us out the moment we stepped off a train. . . . In about a week we arrived at Cherbourg, our port of embarkation. By this time we were not five but more than a hundred, for in every big city where we changed trains we were joined by others also bound for America.[4]

In the 1890s western European governments set up medical stations at the ports to examine immigrants before allowing them to board ship. Germany and Austria also set up medical stations at their eastern borders to check immigrants before allowing them to travel through their lands.

In earlier times, diseased travelers had boarded

ships and spread infection to other passengers. Over 7,000 immigrants died of typhus on the Atlantic crossing in 1847; nearly 1,500 died of cholera in 1853. Immigrants had also spread contagion in Europe; in 1892, cholera was brought into Germany by Russian immigrants making their way to the sea.

Immigrants feared they would be turned back if they showed any sign of illness. Mary Antin, on her way from Russia to Hamburg, recalled the scene of anxiety and confusion at a health station in Germany in 1894:

> In a great lonely field opposite a solitary wooden house with a large yard, our train pulled up at last, and a conductor commanded the passengers to make haste and get out. . . . Here a great many men and women, dressed in white, received us, the women attending to the women and girls of the passengers, and the men to the others.
>
> This was another scene of bewildering confusion, parents losing their children, and little ones crying; baggage being thrown together in one corner of the yard. . . . those white-clad Germans shouting commands, always accompanied with "Quick! Quick!". . .
>
> And no wonder if in some minds stories arose of people being captured by robbers, murderers and the like. Here we had been taken to a lonely place where only that house was to be seen; our things were taken away,

our friends separated from us; a man came to inspect us, as if to ascertain our full value; strange-looking people driving us about like dumb animals, helpless and unresisting . . . driven into a little room where a great kettle was boiling on a little stove; our clothes taken off, our bodies rubbed with a slippery substance that might be any bad thing; a shower of warm water let down on us without warning; again driven to another little room where we sit, wrapped in woolen blankets till large, coarse bags are brought in, their contents turned out, and we see only a cloud of steam, and hear the women's orders to dress ourselves. . . . We are forced to pick out our clothes from among all the others, with the steam blinding us; we choke, cough, entreat the women to give us time; they persist "Quick! Quick, or you'll miss the train!" Oh, so we really won't be murdered! They are only making us ready for the continuing of our journey, cleaning us of all suspicions of dangerous germs.[5]

In 1891, the United States had passed a law excluding immigrants who showed symptoms of certain "loathsome or contagious diseases." Two of these diseases were widely spread in eastern Europe. They were favus, a fungus that caused the skin, especially the scalp, to break into scabs; and trachoma, which attacked the eyes and could lead to blindness. A large percentage of the immigrants who were turned back suffered from one of these two diseases. An immigrant wrote to the Yiddish-American newspaper, the *Jewish Daily Forward,* in 1910:

> I have been in America for several years, with my father and three sisters. We left Mother and two younger sisters back home. We kept sending money to them and hoped for the time when Mother and our two sisters could come here too.
> Finally they started out. Suddenly we got a letter from Mother telling us that on the way one of our sisters, eighteen years of age, was detained because she had trachoma in her eyes, and they all turned back home.
> Now we want to write our mother that she should leave our sister at home for a time and come here with the other sister. Though we all feel guilty at the thought of leaving our sister alone, we question whether it is right for the whole family to suffer because of one.[6]

More difficulties were to come. "We were land-folk and frightened of the sea,"[7] wrote Stoyan Christowe. The Atlantic was large, storms were common, shipwrecks not beyond possibility. Mary Marchak, emigrating from Poland with her mother in 1913, recalled:

We were two or three days out of Danzig, and it happened about three o'clock in the morning. They say we hit an iceberg. There was an awful jar. It threw me right out of bed. And then the sailors were knocking on everybody's cabin telling them to go up, go up. We were on the bottom deck, so we had to go all the way up. The deck was just full. It was dark, foggy, and you couldn't see a thing. And everybody was crying and carrying on. And I saw tears in my mother's eyes. She put a rosary in my hand and she said, "You pray, honey. You pray." Everybody was hollering. And they're pulling somebody back because he was going to jump overboard. And the men were running back and forth, and getting the lifeboats and sliding them down on ropes. And the people were trying to get saved. Oh, and that noise, booing—the ship's foghorn—Dooouoo! that was in my ears for the longest time. Another ship rescued us, but most of our belongings like bedding and things were lost on the ship that was wrecked. The only thing we still had with us was a wicker basket.[8]

After the turn of the century, ocean liners like the one Mary Marchak started on introduced a new class of accommodations for immigrants traveling cheaply—third-class cabins, which slept six or eight passengers. But most immigrants who arrived before

1914 traveled on older ships. Men, women, and children were crammed into steerage—tight, damp spaces in large holds below deck, where bunks rose up in tiers.

But steerage conditions on the steamships which had started to ply the Atlantic in the 1850s were better than the conditions on the sailing ships that had carried earlier immigrants to America. The holds were larger and better ventilated, and the voyage was shortened from about six weeks to ten to fifteen days. But it was only in comparison to the sailing vessels that conditions on the steamships were better. A report of the International Emigration Commission in 1921 described one ship:

> Large numbers of emigrants are crowded together in a comparatively small space. . . . 32 [bunks] and more are placed close together, forming a compact mass with narrow passages between.
>
> As regards ventilation, the port-holes—if any exist—have to be shut at least on one side when there is the slightest sea running; while the lighting is so insufficient that it is sometimes necessary to use artificial light in the middle of the day. . . .
>
> Part of the accommodation is often used as a dining room, and this makes conditions still worse on account of the bad ventilation. In bad weather, when passengers are seasick, the position becomes intolerable.[9]

An investigator for the U.S. Immigration Commission posed as a Czech peasant and sailed in steerage on a typical immigrant ship in 1911. She later wrote:

When the steerage is full, each passenger's space is limited to his berth, which then serves as bed, clothes and towel rack, cupboard, and baggage space. . . . There was no hook on which to hang a garment, no receptacle for refuse . . . no cans for use in case of seasickness. . . .

The one wash room, about 7 by 9 feet, contained 10 faucets of cold salt water . . . and as many basins. . . . This same basin served as a dishpan for greasy tins, as a laundry tub for soiled handkerchiefs and clothing, and as a basin for shampoos, and without receiving any special cleaning. It was the only receptacle to be found in case of seasickness. . . . No woman with the smallest degree of modesty, and with no other conveniences than a wash room, used jointly with men, and a faucet of cold salt water can keep clean amidst such surroundings for a period of twelve days and more. . . .

[The eating utensils] consist of a fork, a large spoon, and a combination workingman's tin lunch pail. The bottom or pail part is used for soup and frequently as a wash basin; a small tin dish that fits into the top of the pail is used for meat and potatoes; a cylindrical projection on the lid is a dish for vegetables or stewed fruits; a tin cup that fits onto this projection is for drinks. These must serve the passenger throughout the voyage. . . . The dishes are soon rusty, and not fit to eat from.

The investigator summed up her steerage experience:

During these twelve days in the steerage I lived in a disorder and in surroundings that offended every sense. Only the fresh breeze from the sea overcame the sickening odors. The vile language of the men, the screams of the women . . . the crying of the children, . . . and practically every sound that reached the ear, irritated beyond endurance. . . . Everything was dirty, sticky, and disagreeable to the touch. Every impression was offensive.[10]

Immigrants still managed to have good times on board. On clear days and nights, they came up to the deck, where they could sun, read, talk, dance, play cards, and spin fantasies about America.

Then came the excitement of the first sight of their goal. Anzia Yezierska, who came from Russia in 1901, described a scene that was repeated on ship after ship:

"Land! land!" came the joyous shout. All crowded and pushed on deck. They strained and stretched to get the first glimpse of the "golden country," lifting their children on their shoulders that they might see. . . . Men fell on their knees to pray. Women hugged their babies and wept. Children danced. Strangers embraced and kissed like old friends. Old men and old women had in their eyes a look of young people in love. . . . America! America![11]

But one more trial awaited the immigrants—examination by the U.S. Bureau of Immigration. Eighty percent landed in New York. Until 1855 there had been no receiving station in New York. Then New York state opened an immigrant depot at an old fort called Castle Garden at the tip of Manhattan. The main purpose was to protect immigrants from the hustlers and thieves who preyed on the newcomers at the docks. Here, immigrants could safely change money, buy train and boat tickets, get information on lodging. Ellis Island, run by the U.S. Immigration Bureau, replaced Castle Garden in 1892. It was not only for the immigrants' protection however; it would screen out "undesirables."

As great waves of immigrants from the poorest parts of Europe poured into the United States, "older" Americans began to protest. They claimed that the poverty and backwardness of the newcomers would debase American life. They said that low-paid immigrant laborers brought down the wages of American workers. They charged that immigrant neighborhoods were hotbeds of crime and disease. They asked for laws to regulate the flow into the country. Laws were gradually passed, and Ellis Island was where they were applied.

People in poor health were excluded. Criminals and anarchists were barred. Penniless newcomers would be turned back, but so would those who had contracted jobs in America before they came, for an 1885 law made it illegal to import foreign labor. In 1917, a literacy test weeded out the uneducated, and an intelligence test screened out those with learning or mental disabilities.

Although only about 11 percent were held at Ellis Island for further evaluation, and only about 2 percent were ultimately refused admission, many immigrants were fearful. They were lined up, herded here and there around a huge hall, poked and probed by health examiners, asked a stream of questions by immigration inspectors.

Immigrants were led in a long line past two doctors. One looked for any physical or mental abnormality. The other checked for contagious diseases. Anyone appearing unfit received a chalk mark on the right shoulder. The immigrants so marked would be held for a more thorough examination. Nina Goodenov recalled:

> My mother was very weak, and she was examined and set aside. Then we had to follow a line into another place where we were given something to eat, and I was walking behind my mother and noticed on the back of

her jacket a white cross. I realized that it meant that she was going to be deported. I don't know what gave me the idea, but I saw those white crosses on other people.

As I walked with her I had enough sense to put my hand on her shoulder and little by little wipe that cross off, and so they let her through. There were several people marked like that who did not get to the place where we got. They were deported, they were sent back. . . .

As far as Ellis Island was concerned, it was a nightmare. After all, none of us spoke English. We had no idea where we were going and no idea what was to be done to us. We had no idea what they wanted of us. There were hundreds and hundreds of people and they were treated exactly like sheep. "Go here. Go sit here. Wait here. Wait there." It took a day and a night. You had no place to sleep. You had to sleep on the benches, just sitting up.[12]

Louis Adamic recalled:

The examiner sat bureaucratically—very much in the manner of officials in the Old Country—behind a great desk, which stood on a high platform. . . . [He] spoke a bewildering mixture of many Slavic languages. He had a stern voice and a sour visage. I had difficulty understanding some of his questions. . . .

When and where was I born? My nationality? Religion? Was I a legitimate child? What were the names of my parents? Was I an imbecile? Was I a prostitute? (I assume that male and female immigrants were subject to the same questionnaire.) Was I an ex-convict? A criminal? Why had I come to the United States?

I was questioned as to the state of my finances and I produced the required twenty-five dollars.

What did I expect to do in the United States? I replied that I hoped to get a job. What kind of job? I didn't know; any kind of job.

. . ."And who is this person . . . who is meeting you here?" I answered that Stefan Radin was the brother of a friend of mine. . . .

. . . Steve Radin was called into the examining-room and asked, in English, to state his relation to me.

He answered, of course, that he was not related to me at all.

Whereupon the inspector fairly pounced upon me, speaking the dreadful botch of Slavic languages. What did I mean by lying to him? He said a great many other things which I did not understand. I did comprehend, however, his threat to return me to the Old Country. It appeared that America had no room for liars: America was glad to welcome to its shores only decent, honest, truthful people.

My heart pounded.[13]

Realizing that the official had made a mistake, Radin and Adamic were able to clear up the misunderstanding, and Adamic was released from Ellis Island.

Defenders of the system at Ellis Island argued that there was no way to process the huge number of immigrants without procedures that might strike the newcomers as cold and harsh. The immigration station often had to handle numbers far beyond its resources. In 1907, when the number of arrivals reached a record level, over one million came through Ellis Island. There could be fifteen thousand in a day, yet the facilities were designed to handle only five thousand per day.

Ellis Island remained the gateway to the United States until 1943. After that, American consulates overseas cleared immigrants for entry.

Sixteen million immigrants passed through Ellis Island during its fifty-year existence as an immigration station. Most eastern European immigrants entered the United States in just this way. They were tired and battered after their journey. Many wondered whether they had done the right thing. Many were pained at being uprooted from the people and places they knew and loved. But as they passed successfully through Ellis Island, they also felt relief. They had made it. They had completed a great adventure, and they were now starting their second adventure—life in America.

Chapter 6

All That Glittered Was Not Gold

I looked about the narrow streets of squeezed-in stores and houses, ragged clothes, dirty bedding oozing out of the windows, ash-cans and garbage-cans cluttering the sidewalks. . . . "Where are the green fields and open spaces in America?" cried my heart. "Where is the golden country of my dreams."[1]

ANZIA YEZIERSKA

America was hard on eastern European immigrants. It offered them the worst jobs, the lowest wages, the most wretched living quarters. Most of the immigrants never rose up from this bottom level. They lived and died there. The promise of America, the dream, would only begin to be realized by their children and grandchildren.

A small percentage of eastern Europeans made their way to America's farmlands. A good number

92

of the Czechs who came in the 1850s and 1860s pioneered and homesteaded in the Mid- and Southwest. In the late nineteenth century, Croatians became California growers, planting orchards and vineyards of apples, apricots, plums, figs, and grapes. In the early twentieth century, Poles bought abandoned farms in Connecticut that had been thought to be worked out. They planted tobacco and onions and through hard work made the forsaken fields bloom again.

But these farmers were not typical. Most eastern Europeans remained in the East coast port cities where they landed or traveled inland only to reach other industrial centers. They arrived poor and desperate. Most of their money had been spent on the journey. They had to find work fast. They took any jobs that were open to unskilled immigrants who could not speak English.

After the Civil War, America's industrial revolution swung into high gear. Machines performed more and more of the processes of production. Human labor was less and less valued. Wages were as low as employers could get away with paying. The great throngs of immigrants who arrived having to work *at* anything, *for* anything, or starve, suited industry's needs perfectly. Many jobs did not require complicated skills. All they demanded was physical strength and endurance. These qualities were all that the immigrants had to sell.

Between 1880 and 1920, one of every three people employed in manufacture in the United States was an immigrant. In cities with large immigrant populations—New York, Chicago, Detroit, Pittsburgh, among others—the proportion of immigrant industrial workers was more than twice as high. Coal mining depended almost entirely on immigrant labor.

Immigrant workers experienced all the ills of an industrial age largely unregulated by law or social conscience. They worked ten-, twelve-, fourteen-, even sixteen-hour days. Their work places were unsanitary, unhealthy, and unsafe. Their low wages insured that none but an exceptional few would rise above poverty. In an era of industrial exploitation of labor, immigrants fared the worst. The historian Oscar Handlin compared earnings around the year 1900:

> It was characteristic that, about then, for every hundred dollars earned by native wage earners, the Italian-born earned eighty-four, the Hungarians sixty-eight, and other Europeans fifty-four.[2]

These "other Europeans" were overwhelmingly from eastern Europe.

More than half of the eastern European Jews in the United States during this era worked in clothing manufacture, which was based in a few major cities, New York and Chicago in particular. The other eastern Europeans—Hungarians and Slavs—dispersed more widely. They went to the textile mills of New England, the coal mines and steel mills of

Pennsylvania and Ohio, the stockyards and packing houses of Chicago, Kansas City, and Omaha, the automobile plants of Detroit, the railroad construction camps of the Mid- and Northwest, the docks of a dozen busy ports. But whatever the industry, and whatever the locale, they found the same circumstances over and over: brutal exploitation of their labor and hideous living conditions.

Homestead, Pennsylvania, was the site of the Carnegie Steel Company. Andrew Carnegie earned twenty-five million dollars a year from his industrial empire. The journalist Hamlin Garland described how Carnegie's employees lived in 1892:

> The streets were horrible; the buildings were poor; the sidewalks were sunken and full of holes; . . . everywhere the yellow mud of the streets lay kneaded into sickly masses, through which groups of pale, lean men slouched in faded garments, grimy with the soot and dirt of the mills. The town was as squalid as could be imagined, and the people . . . discouraged and sullen.[3]

Inside the plant, according to another observer:

> Everywhere in the enormous sheds were pits gaping like the mouth of hell, and ovens emitting a terrible degree of heat, with grimy men filling and lining them. One man jumps down, works desperately for a few minutes, and is then pulled up, exhausted. Another

immediately takes his place; there is no hesitation.[4]

The unskilled day laborers of Homestead earned fourteen cents an hour, a little less than ten dollars a week. They worked twelve hours a day, seven days a week. Nearly thirty years later, a Russian steelworker's summary of his workweek in Pittsburgh in 1919 told how little conditions in the industry had changed:

> Time on the job, 91 hours; eating about 9; street car (45 minutes each way), 10.5; sleep (7½ hours a day), 52.5; dressing, undressing, washing, and so forth, 5; that totals 168 or every single hour in the week, and it's how I slave.[5]

A study of the steel industry in 1920 summarized the situation of the immigrant worker:

> Nine times out of ten he is a peasant, taking an industrial job for the first time. . . . If the mill is shut down, he is the first to be laid off; if the job is unusually hot, greasy, or heavy, he is the first to be set to it. He is the most arbitrarily, often brutally, shifted and ordered about. . . . He is the most likely to be kept beyond his tour with no additional pay.[6]

Across Pennsylvania from the steel mills in the west lie the anthracite coal fields in the east. A U.S.

Department of Labor report described the houses available to immigrant workers in the coal towns:

> Many of the houses rented from the mining companies had fallen into a state of extreme disrepair because the companies had refused or neglected to attend to them. In one such house the beams had given way under the kitchen floor, leaving it unusable and the walls warped. The cellar and the parlor were damp all the time and flooded when it rained. The chimneys were bad. The roof leaked. The plank walks in the yard were rotted and broken. The company had made no repairs in this house for two years.[7]

The stockyards district of Chicago—around the slaughterhouses and meat-packing plants—was notorious. A social worker made the following observations in 1924:

> When I came to my field in Chicago, I found forty thousand human beings huddled into a half-square-mile area. Here dwelt a sturdy, thrifty, industrious people grimly battling their way out of the depths to gain for themselves and their children a better place to live. Poles, Bohemians, Lithuanians, Slovaks, Germans, and Irish numbered their thousands. . . . Their sky was constantly overcast by black clouds belched forth from the smoking stacks of Chicago's giant packing industries. The air was

polluted by a nauseating stench from cattle pens, slaughter houses, and fertilizer plants, and poisoned by foul gases which came from putrifying offal dumped into that wide, sluggish open sewer called Bubbly Creek. Sickly grass, scrubby trees, and dirty babies were making pitiful attempts to grow. In one precinct, of every five babies born, three had died before they were a year old.[8]

Men who came to the United States as Birds of Passage wanted to invest little of their earnings in housekeeping in the United States in order to save for their return home. They usually lived in boarding-houses or apartments or rented an apartment communally. Sometimes they purchased bed and board from a fellow-immigrant who operated a boarding-house. Many of the "Birds" eventually stayed in the United States. They married immigrant women or sent home for wives and fiancées to join them and set up house in America. But their first few years in the United States might very well have been spent in an arrangement like the following apartment, or "flat," as it is called here, near the Chicago stock-yards. It was described by the writer and reformer Upton Sinclair in his novel *The Jungle* in 1906:

> [It was] a four-room flat in one of that wilder-ness of two-story frame tenements that lie "back of the yards." There were four such flats in each building, and each of the four was

a "boarding house" for the occupancy of foreigners—Lithuanians, Poles, Slovaks, or Bohemians. . . . There would be an average of half a dozen boarders to each room—sometimes there were thirteen or fourteen to one room, fifty or sixty to a flat. Each one of the occupants furnished his own accommodations —that is, a mattress and some bedding. The mattresses would be spread upon the floor in rows— and there would be nothing else in the place except a stove. It was by no means unusual for two men to own the same mattress in common, one working by day and using it by night, and the other working at night and using it in the daytime.[9]

The stockyard flats were probably the worst in the country. But boarding arrangements elsewhere weren't much better. In 1914, a Massachusetts immigration commission issued a report on the living arrangements of young immigrant women who had come to Boston without families:

In a dilapidated tenement, where the rain comes in through the walls and ceiling, a family of seven have an apartment of four rooms, with two men lodgers and one woman. There is one toilet in the basement for the thirty-two persons who live in the building. The girl is eighteen and speaks very little English, although she has been here two years.

She has not been to night school [to learn
English] because she has been afraid "of being
treated badly by the men." . . .

A Lithuanian girl has lived for four years
in a family of three who have four rooms and
eight lodgers, five men and three women. This
girl works as a stitcher in a tailor shop. She
started to go to night school when she first
came, but the landlady objected as she wanted
her to help with the housework in the evenings. . . .

A Polish girl of eighteen who has been in
America four months, having borrowed her
passage money from her brother in this
country, is lodging with a family of four who
live in four rooms with five lodgers, three men
and two women. This girl is working seven
days a week, washing cars in the railroad
yards in Boston.[10]

A report of the Children's Bureau of the U.S.
Department of Labor told how children grew up
amid the industrial wastes of the Pennsylvania coal
region:

Few places offer so little opportunity for education through play as did the town of Shenan-
doah. The houses set flush with the sidewalks
were crowded on the lots so that there was
hardly a yard in the city. . . . The town had no
parks. . . . The little children went wading in
the black streams which flowed along two sides

of the borough and received the sewage and refuse of the mines. . . . Children played on the dumps of refuse and garbage and climbed to the tops of mountains of [coal].[11]

For many children of immigrants, the play years were short. They were sent to work, for their families needed the income they could contribute. In Pennsylvania, boys were apprenticed to the coal mines as early as the age of nine. Their mining careers began in the "breakers," which the social reformer John Spargo described in 1906:

> Work in the coal breakers is exceedingly hard and dangerous. Crouched over the chutes, the boys sit hour after hour picking out the pieces of slate and other refuse from the coal as it rushes past to the washers. From the cramped position they have to assume, most of them become more or less deformed and bent-backed like old men. . . .
>
> The coal is hard, and accidents to the hands, such as cut, broken, or crushed fingers, are common among the boys. Sometimes there is a worse accident: a terrified shriek is heard, and a boy is mangled and torn in the machinery, or disappears in the chute to be picked out later smothered and dead. Clouds of dust fill the breakers and are inhaled by the boys, laying the foundation for asthma and miners' consumption.
>
> I once stood in a breaker for half an hour

and tried to do the work a twelve-year-old boy was doing day after day, for ten hours at a stretch, for sixty cents a day. . . . Outside the sun shone brightly. . . . Within the breaker there was blackness, clouds of deadly dust enfolded everything, the harsh, grinding . . . machinery and the ceaseless rushing of coal through the chutes filled the ears.[12]

In New York City, children worked beside their immigrant parents in the tenement apartments that served as home and shop to many a family. Home manufacture became a prevalent mode of production in the cigar and clothing industries in the late nineteenth century. Samuel Gompers, an English-Jewish immigrant who was president of the Cigarmakers' Union before he took on the leadership of the American Federation of Labor, explained how the home workshop evolved in the cigar trade:

In 1871 and 1872 many Bohemians moved into downtown New York. The Bohemians did not find it easy to learn English or to adjust themselves to New York life. As many manufacturers thought they had a . . . system under which practically unskilled workers could produce cigars, soon they added the tenement feature. . . . The manufacturers bought or rented a block of tenements and subrented the apartments to cigar makers who with their families lived and worked in three or four rooms. The cigar makers paid rent to their employer for living room which was their work space, bought from him their supplies, furnished their own tools, received in return a small wage for completed work. . . . The whole family—old and young had to work in order to earn a livelihood—work early and late, Sunday as well as Monday.[13]

Danish-born Jacob Riis, journalist and social reformer, visited some of the Bohemian tenement cigarmakers in New York in 1890.

Take a row of houses in East Tenth Street as an instance. They contained thirty-five families of cigarmakers. . . . This room with two windows giving on the street, and a rear attachment without windows, called a bedroom by courtesy, is rented at $12.25 a month. In the front room man and wife work at the bench from six in the morning till nine at night. They make a team, stripping the tobacco leaves together; then he makes the filler, and she rolls the wrapper on and finishes the cigar. For a thousand they receive $3.75, and can turn out together three thousand cigars a week. . . . Three bright little children play about the floor.

His neighbor on the same floor . . . with $11.75 rent to pay for like accommodation . . . has the advantage of his oldest boy's work besides his wife's at the bench. Three properly make a team, and these three can turn out four thousand cigars a week, at $3.75. This Bohemian has a large family; there are four children, too small to work, to be cared for.[14]

The most notorious tenement factories were the garment sweatshops of the Jewish Lower East Side in New York. Jacob Riis visited these as well.

Take the Second Avenue Elevated Railroad at Chatham Square and ride up half a mile through the sweaters' district. Every open window of the big tenements . . . gives you a glimpse of one of these shops as the train speeds by. Men and women bending over their machines, or ironing clothes at the window. . . . The road is like a big gangway through an endless work-room where vast multitudes are forever laboring. Morning, noon, or night, it makes no difference; the scene is always the same.[15]

"Sweaters" bought or rented sewing machines, installed them in tenement apartments, and then contracted work from clothing manufacturers. The manufacturers supplied the sweaters with precut pieces of garments, such as shirt fronts and backs, or sleeves and cuffs. The sweatshops assembled and finished the garments. The labor force of a sweatshop would consist of the sweater, his family, boarders who lived there with him, and day workers who lived nearby. There might be up to twenty workers in the two or three small, dark rooms who worked sixteen hours a day.

Competition among sweaters was keen. They had to bid against other sweaters for a manufacturer's business. The sweaters who could produce the most garments at the least cost to the manufacturer were the ones who walked away with the contracts. In turn, the workers they kept on in their shops were the ones who accepted the lowest pay. It was a system of exploitation down the line, each level squeezing the one below. Jacob Riis wrote:

Up two flights of stairs, three, four, . . . whirring sewing machines behind closed doors betraying what goes on within, to the door that opens. . . . A sweater, this, in a small way. Five men and a woman, two young girls, not fifteen, and a boy who says unasked that he is fifteen, and lies in saying it, are at the machines sewing knickerbockers, "knee-pants" in the Ludlow Street dialect. The floor is littered ankle-deep with half-sewn garments. In the alcove, on a couch of many dozens of "pants" ready for the finisher, a bare-legged baby with pinched face is asleep. . . . The faces, hands, and arms to the elbows of everyone in the room are black with the color of the cloth on which they are working. . . .

They are "learners," all of them, says the woman, who proves to be the wife of the boss, and have "come over" only a few weeks ago. . . . How much do they earn? . . . The workers . . . say indifferently, as though the question were of no interest: from two to five dollars [a week]. . . . They work no longer than to nine o'clock at night, from daybreak.[16]

At the lowest level were those families who subcontracted from the sweaters. The poet Edwin Markham wrote about these families in 1907:

In unaired rooms, mothers and fathers sew by day and by night. Those in the home sweatshop must work cheaper than those in the factory sweatshops if they would drain work from the factory, which already has skinned the wage down to a miserable pittance. . . .

All the year in New York and in other cities you may watch children radiating to and from such pitiful homes. Nearly any hour on the East Side of New York City you can see them —pallid boy and spindling girl—their faces dulled, their backs bent under a heavy load of garments piled on head and shoulders, . . . Once at home with the sewing, the little worker sits close to the inadequate window, struggling with the snarls of thread or shoving the needle through the unyielding cloth. Even if by happy chance the small worker goes to school, the sewing which he puts down at the last moment in the morning waits for his return.

. . . A child may add to the family purse from 50 cents to $1.50 a week. . . . A little child of [seven] can be very useful in threading needles, in cutting the loose threads at the ends of seams, and in pulling out bastings. . . .

In New York City alone, 60,000 children are shut up in the home sweatshops. This is a conservative estimate.[17]

Such living and working conditions took a toll on the health of children and adults. Overwork, overcrowding, and poor sanitation made immigrants susceptible to tuberculosis, a dreaded disease at that time. By 1906, it affected twelve out of every thousand Jews on the Lower East Side. It was called the "Jewish disease" and the "tailor's disease."

Each industry, each locale had its hazards. Asthma and lung disorders afflicted miners. Burns were common around the blazing furnaces and molten metals of the steel mills. The daily labor itself took its toll, as a Russian steelworker in Philadelphia explained around 1920:

> The boss makes two of us carry steel which should require four. If I refuse, I lose my job. Lots of weeks the work is so heavy I get pains in my back and have to lay off three days out of seven.[18]

In *The Jungle,* Upton Sinclair dissected the living and working conditions in the Chicago stockyards at the beginning of this century. Sinclair's exposé of the muck and filth in the food processing plants created a great public alarm, and helped bring about

the passage of the Pure Food and Drug Act and the
Beef Inspection Act within six months of the novel's
publication. Here is part of Sinclair's catalogue of
the hazards stockyards workers suffered:

> Let a man so much as scrape his finger pushing
> a truck in the pickle rooms, and he might have
> a sore that would put him out of the world; all
> the joints in his fingers might be eaten by the
> acid, one by one. Of the butchers and floors-
> men, the beef boners and trimmers, and all
> those who used knives, you could scarcely find
> a person who had the use of his thumb; time
> and time again the base of it had been slashed,
> till it was a mere lump of flesh against which
> the man pressed the knife to hold it. The hands
> of these men would be criss-crossed with cuts,
> until you could no longer pretend to count
> them or to trace them. They would have no
> nails,—they had worn them off pulling hides.
> . . . There were men who worked in the cook-
> ing rooms, in the midst of steam and sickening
> odors . . . in these rooms the germs of tubercu-
> losis [carried by diseased livestock] might live
> for two years, but the supply was renewed
> every hour. . . . There were those who worked
> in the chilling rooms and whose special disease
> was rheumatism; the time limit that a man
> could work in the chilling rooms was said to
> be five years. . . . There were those who made
> the tins for the canned meat, and their hands,

too, were a maze of cuts, and each cut represented a chance for blood poisoning. Some worked at the stamping machines, and it was very seldom that one could work long there at the pace that was set, and not give out and forget himself, and have a part of his hand chopped off. . . . As for the other men, who worked in the tank rooms full of steam, and in some of which there were open vats near the level of the floor, their peculiar trouble was that they fell into the vats; and when they were fished out, there was never enough of them to be worth exhibiting—sometimes they would be overlooked for days, till all but the bones of them had gone out to the world as Durham's Pure Leaf Lard![19]

Few workers carried insurance, and industry compensated its casualties inadequately, if at all. The historian Kenneth D. Miller wrote:

The experience of Josef Leksa, a Slovak immigrant, is typical of a shockingly large number of Slavic immigrants who have entered our industrial world. Coming to America when he was nineteen . . . Leksa soon secured a position in a coal mine. . . . One day the miners working down below in the shaft heard a crash. Running up, they found young Leksa pinned under a huge mass of coal and rock. There had been a "fall." He was taken to a hospital, where it was soon discovered that if he recovered at all, he would be a cripple for life. While his life was still in the balance, he was visited by a lawyer who presented him with a paper to sign, which he understood to be a claim against the company for damages. After several months Leska left the hospital on crutches, hopelessly maimed. When he went to the company offices to see about his claim, he was confronted with the paper he had signed, and told that it was an agreement to settle with the company for $200. In vain did he protest and appeal to the courts for redress. The company paid him $200 and sent him away.

Some months later he was found on the streets of New York, begging. . . . "Why should I go back and be a burden upon my folks?" he protested. "It was America that crippled me, and America should take care of me. I'll never let the folks at home know what has happened to me. I always write that I am well and happy."[20]

The ignorance of the immigrants was one of their major handicaps: their ignorance of the English language, of their legal rights, of private and government agencies that might help them. America often took advantage of this. A Chicago social worker in 1908 described how employment agencies exploited immigrants' ignorance and their desperation to find work. These agencies assembled work gangs for other locations.

Men are employed for this kind of work not
as individuals, but in groups of thirty or more,
and are sent to parts of the country of which
they are entirely ignorant. . . .

The maximum "registration fee" which the
employment agent may charge is fixed by
statute at two dollars. . . . [But] an investigator
. . . was told frankly, "We charge all we can
get."

Fees are higher when the applicant is unable
to speak English.

Sometimes the labor gangs were sent to nonexistent
jobs, or to jobs very different from what had been
described to them.

During the past year a railroad has been building from Searcey in north-central Arkansas to
Leslie, about ninety miles farther west. Great
numbers of men were sent from Chicago to
Leslie to work on this road. . . . One of these
[groups] was made up of Hungarians. They
were fifty-three men and two women—one of
these had a baby—who expected to act as
cooks for the gang. . . . They paid the Chicago
agent fourteen dollars apiece and were
promised steady work at $1.40 a day. When
they reached Leslie . . . they were told that
the work was twenty-five miles from there.
They walked to this place but the foreman only
laughed at them and said he had no work for
any such number. He finally put to work

fifteen men and the woman who was unem-
cumbered with the baby. The rest were told
that there would be work for them later on but
they were without money or food and so could
not stay. They started to walk back to Chicago
where more such jobs are always to be had![21]

Employers believed that progress in industry
meant improving technology and reducing the cost
of production. It did not mean improving working
conditions or wages. It was this attitude, more than
anything else, that turned the immigrants' American
dream into a nightmare. For example, although New
York passed a law prohibiting manufacture in homes
in 1892, it took about fifteen years for the law to
be enforced. Gradually garment manufacture shifted
from the tenement shop to the factory loft. Immigrants received some benefit from this shift, but the
greater advantage was to the manufacturer. The
novelist and journalist Ernest Poole compared the
factory system with the tenement sweatshop in a
1903 magazine article:

> Endless saving, dividing, narrowing labor—
> this is the factory. Down either side of the
> long factory table forty operators bend over
> machines, and each one sews the twentieth part
> of a coat. One man makes hundreds of pockets.
> On sewing pockets his whole working life is
> narrowed. . . . The coat passes down the long
> bench, then through the hands of a dozen

pressers and basters and finishers—each doing one minute part swiftly, with exact precision. Through thirty hands it comes out at last fourteen minutes quicker, four cents cheaper; the factory had beaten the task shop.

And the human cost—is it, too, reduced? Is the worker better off here than he was in the sweatshop? . . . Wages by the week for the most skilled workers are slightly higher in the factory than they were in the sweatshop. They are lower for the unskilled majority. This majority must slowly increase, for the factory system progresses by transferring skill to machinery. Hours are shorter; work is less irregular; the shop is sanitary; the air is more wholesome—but the pocketmaker is often as exhausted by 6:00 P.M. as the coatmaker was at 10:00 P.M., for his work is more minute, more intense, more monotonous

There was, however, one effect of the shift to the factory that did promise long-term benefits. Poole explained:

Still, the workers have gained most decidedly. The factory is a help to the union. Through the past twenty years labor unions were formed again and again, only to be broken by new waves of ignorant immigrants. In the system of small scattered shops the unions had no chance. . . . All this is ended.[22]

How workers put this to use will be seen in chapter 8.

If the way they were made to work was a reminder of the immigrants' failed dreams, so was the way they were made to live. Marcus Ravage recalled the Lower East Side when he arrived there in December 1900:

> I have not forgotten and I never can forget that first pungent breath of the slums which were to become my home for the next five years. . . . I know that the idea prevalent among Americans is that the alien imports his slums with him to the detriment of his adopted country, that the squalor and the misery and the filth of the foreign quarters in the large cities of the United States are characteristic of the native life of those people who live in those quarters. But that is an error and a slander. The slums are emphatically not of our making. So far is the immigrant from being accustomed to such living conditions that the first thing that repels him on his arrival in New York is the realization of the dreadful level of life to which his fellows have sunk. . . .
>
> I shall never forget how depressed my heart became as I trudged through those littered streets, with the rows of pushcarts lining the sidewalks and the centers of the thoroughfares, the ill-smelling merchandise, and the deafening noise. . . . So this was America, I kept thinking. This was the boasted American freedom and

opportunity—the freedom for respectable citizens to sell cabbages from hideous carts, the opportunity to live in those monstrous, dirty caves that shut out the sunshine.[23]

In their homelands, the peasants of eastern Europe were doomed to ever-increasing poverty, and the Jews to gradual extinction. For many immigrants it boiled down to a choice between two kinds of poverty, two kinds of oppression. Over the long run, in America, there was far greater hope. Some immigrants realized their hopes soon. Some were fortunate or clever enough to achieve clear improvements in their living and working conditions within a few years of their arrival. Many did not achieve such gains themselves, but saw their children graduate from American schools and move into better neighborhoods and more rewarding jobs. Since the immigrants started in America at the bottom, there was nowhere to go but up. And in America, it was more possible to move up than anywhere else in the world at that time.

Some immigrants were modestly successful quite soon. In 1914, Mary Boreth, her sister, and her mother, came to America to join the father who had come a year earlier. There was a pleasant home waiting for them in Roebling, New Jersey, where Mary's father had found work. The family took in boarders to supplement the father's income, but they considered themselves immensely better off than they had been in Hungary.

The town of Roebling was named for John A. Roebling who had a factory which manufactured wire rope. The John A. Roebling Company was famous for having built the Brooklyn Bridge in New York and the Golden Gate Bridge in San Francisco. Roebling also built the town around the factory and rented houses to the workers. The rent was very reasonable.

The house had six rooms with a bathroom and bathtub. We thought it was very beautiful, and very different from what we had been accustomed to—especially the bathtub. We went to school. My father worked. My mother kept boarders and raised the children. In those years there was a very happy feeling.[24]

Mary Asia's family, which came to Milwaukee from the Ukraine in 1897, pooled their savings and their talents to open a dry goods store.

Sam was a whirlwind of energy. He rented the place on East Water Street; had it freshly painted, bought stock, and, in a few weeks, we were moving along briskly. As Sam had assured Papa, the location was good for a dry goods store, and we had many customers, right from the start. The number grew steadily, for everyone liked Sam; and Papa, dignified and quiet, inspired confidence.

Mama, just as she had done in Teofipol, not only took care of the home and young children, but helped in the store, too. She was greatly liked by all our customers, because of her gentleness and sweet ways. . . .

I bought my supplies, and for the opening of my department, I designed twelve hats that were as beautiful and modish as I could make them. Sam arranged them in a fine window display, and success came immediately. . . . Now that I was free to do my own designing, I was happy, even excited over my work. . . . I had no time to brood, or be homesick. I was doing the work I loved and helping to support the family [25]

Golda Meir's mother opened a shop in Milwaukee soon after the family arrived.

Very soon we moved into a little apartment of our own on Walnut Street, in the city's poorer Jewish section. Today that part of Milwaukee is inhabited by blacks who are, for the most part, as poor as we were then. But in 1906 the clapboard houses with their pretty porches and steps looked like palaces to me. I even thought that our flat (which had no electricity and no bathroom) was the height of luxury. . . . Its greatest attraction for my mother [was] a vacant shop that she instantly decided to run. She didn't know one word of English; she had no inkling at all of which products were likely to sell well; she had never run or even worked in a shop before. . . . Fortunately, the women in the neighborhood rallied around her. Many of them were new immigrants themselves, and their natural reaction was to assist another newcomer. They taught her a few English phrases, how to behave behind the counter, how to work the cash register and scales and to whom she could safely allow credit.

. . . Somebody had to mind the store while she was gone. . . . [My older sister] managed to get away from the shop whenever she could, and for months I had to stand behind the counter every morning until mother returned from the market. For an eight- or nine-year-old girl, this was not an easy chore. . . . Coming late to class almost every day was awful, and I used to cry all the way to school. Once a policeman even came to the shop to explain to my mother about truancy. She listened attentively but barely understood anything he said, so I went on being late for school and sometimes never got there at all. . . . My mother— not that she had much alternative—didn't seem to be moved by my bitter resentment of the shop. "We have to live, don't we?" she claimed. . . . "So it will take you a little longer to become a *rebbetzin* (a bluestocking)," she added. I never became a bluestocking, of course, but I learned a lot at that school.[26]

Chapter 7

Many Americas

The alien who comes here from Europe is not the raw material that Americans suppose him to be. He is not a blank sheet to be written on as you see fit. He has not sprung out of nowhere. Quite the contrary. He brings with him a deep-rooted tradition, a system of culture and tastes and habits—a point of view which is as ancient as his national experience. . . . And it is this thing—this entire Old World soul of his—that comes in conflict with America as soon as he has landed.[1]

MARCUS RAVAGE

A 1908 melodrama called *The Melting Pot* expressed the idea that the United States was a melting pot in which all the nationalities of the Old World blended together. For at least fifty years afterward, this view was repeated in political speeches, school

119

textbooks, newspaper editorials, popular books, and films.

But immigrants did not jump into a caldron and let themselves be boiled down into a homogenized American type. They held on to many of their Old World customs and values. They continued to identify with the land of their ancestors at the same time as they became loyal Americans. In the end, it was not one kind of American who emerged from the "pot," but many; not one total, all-encompassing American community, but many Americas.

The places where the immigrants settled became mosaics of immigrant "towns." Here is how one commentator described the ethnic geography of Chicago:

> To the north of the Loop was Germany. To the northwest Poland. To the west were Italy and Israel. To the southwest were Bohemia and Lithuania. And to the south was Ireland.[2]

Smaller communities, like the factory town of Roebling, New Jersey, had a similar composition, as Mary Boreth recalled:

> It was the kind of town where all the Hungarians kept in one group and the Romanians in another. There were also Slovaks, Germans, and Swedes. There were only two Italian families and two Jewish families in the whole town. There were never any problems. They

all got along, but they were separated into little groups.

The Swedes lived further away along the Delaware River and kept to themselves. I don't think they mingled too much with the Hungarians and the Poles. They considered themselves a higher group. But all the rest of us played together—Hungarian, Romanian, Polish, Slovak. All the children of my age went to school together and grew up together.[3]

The Jews of New York's Lower East Side may have looked like an undifferentiated mass to an outsider. But they maintained their ethnic divisions, too, as Marcus Ravage explained:

Though both speak Yiddish, the Jew from Austrian Poland will at first hardly understand his co-religionist from Lithuania. Their dialects differ enormously. . . . And each group entertains a humorous, kindly contempt for the speech and the manners and the foibles of all the others.

. . . It was my lot to settle in that odd bit of world . . . Little Rumania. It was bounded on the east by Clinton Street, with Little Galicia extending on the other side to the East River; by Grand Street on the south, with the Russians and Lithuanians beyond; and on the north lay the . . . vast dark continent of the "real Americans."[4]

In their communities, the immigrants constructed a familiar world in this strange land. They lived with people who spoke their language, followed their religion and customs, shared the same memories of the Old World, and struggled with the same hardships in the New. They provided economic, social, and moral support for each other.

Each immigrant district had its own special vitality. At the Hester Street Market on the Lower East Side, foods and goods were hawked from pushcarts and stands as they had been in Old World village squares. The peddlers were the districts' entrepreneurs, and they supplied the particular needs of their community. A *New York Times* reporter visited the Hester Street Market in 1897:

It is quite unnecessary to go to Europe in order to see a genuine Jewish ghetto. There is one, a large one, the largest in the New World, in fact, right here in New York. . . . The Russian-Jewish inhabitants of the New York ghetto . . . live together in such numbers that they have to a large extent retained their own peculiar modes of life. . . .

Step off a Third Avenue car at the corner of Hester Street and the Bowery some Friday morning and walk east. . . . I say "Friday morning" because the market, striking and characteristic of the ghetto and its life, is held on that day. This is done so that an ample store of eatables may be laid in for *Shabbes* (the Jewish Sabbath) on the morrow. . . .

The pavements along both sides of Hester Street are lined by a continuous double row of pushcarts filled with eatables of every kind agreeable to the palate of the Russian Jew. . . . Here is a cart laden with grapes and pears, and the fruit merchant . . . is shrieking at the top of his voice: *"Gutes frucht! Gutes frucht! Metziehs! Drei pennies die whole lot!"* ("Good fruit! Good fruit! Bargains! Three pennies the whole lot!")

. . . Women and market baskets swarm and push and jostle around some pushcarts at the lower end of the street. . . . It is fish—big fish and little fish, light fish and dark fish, bluefish and whitefish, fresh fish and fish not quite so fresh. . . . These people love fish . . . [for] the Friday evening meal. . . . For fish is good *kosher* (clean) food.[5]

The religion they shared held together this community of Jews from many different lands. It was everywhere apparent: in the kosher foods the immigrants ate, selected, and prepared according to Jewish law; and in the many synagogues tucked in among the tenements. The Jewish religion requires only ten men to form a congregation, and they can assemble anywhere to conduct services. There were several hundred small congregations in the one-mile-square area of the Lower East Side. An 1897 newspaper article described them:

> Few Orthodox* congregations are large enough to afford a separate building for a house of worship. Most of them are small societies made up of fellow townsmen and bearing the name of their native place. Almost every town within the Pale of Jewish settlement in Russia, Austria, or Rumania is represented here by a synagogue. Accordingly, the average congregation must be content with a room and a bedroom on the top floor of some overcrowded tenement house, the smaller room usually being set aside for female worshippers†. . . . As a rule, each synagogue is also a kind of clubhouse, the more devout of the members coming to spend their leisure moments there, reading Psalms, swapping news of the old home, or exchanging notes upon the adopted country.[6]

Religion animated eastern European Christian communities, as well. Immigrants formed parishes led by immigrant priests, and as soon as they could collect the money needed, built their churches. The churches continued to be the center of the immigrants' spiritual, social, and even political life, just

---

* The most strictly observant form of Judaism.
† In Orthodox Jewish synagogues, women worship separately from men.

as they had been in the villages of eastern Europe. The Fiftieth Anniversary Album of the Church of St. Stanislaus Kostka in Chicago, the largest Polish parish in the United States, portrays the development of an immigrant community around its church:

It is a well-known and certain thing . . . wherever there is a priest, a church, wherever a parish is being created, there Polish life grows vigorously, there our number multiplies, for from all sides people come willingly, feeling better among their own and with their own, feeling safer under the protective wings of the parish and with their own shepherd, who here in a foreign land is not only a representative of his brothers before the altar of the Lord but leads and represents them in all worldly affairs.[7]

In partitioned Poland, the Church had been a pillar of nationalism, keeping alive the Polish language, traditions, and national spirit. Churches had been perhaps the only institutions where Poles could assemble as Poles. In the United States, Poles joined a Catholic Church that was dominated by another people, Irish-Americans. The Church hierarchy was largely Irish and opposed the advancement of Polish clergy. It tried to "Americanize" the Polish parishes by turning them over to Irish-American priests. Polish rituals were abandoned and sermons were given in English. All these things angered Polish immigrants who had built the churches with their hard-earned money and who wanted a church they could continue to consider their own. Early in the twentieth century, Father Waclaw Kruszka denounced the Irish influence as he urged that a Pole be elevated to the office of bishop:

> It is an undeniable fact that although the Irish form only about one-third of the Catholic population, of the hundred Catholic bishops in the United States, almost all are of Irish nationality, a few German bishops being only a drop in the sea. . . . From this fact, one can easily deduct the conclusion that the Irish want a certain priest for bishop, just because he is Irish. . . .
>
> Since 1854, the Poles built every year churches, schools, asylums, colleges . . . paid always faithfully their church taxes . . . and during this long period never enjoyed any rights and privileges in the church, never had any representation in the hierarchy. This is evidently unjust and un-American! And now, when we make a just complaint, they say to us, that there was not as yet any Polish priest worthy to become a bishop but as soon as they will find one, they will make one. I need not say that this is a poor excuse, and an uncharitable one, not worthy of a true Christian. It is an open insult to the whole Polish clergy.

Were so long the Irish and the few Germans the only worthy . . . ? One must be arrogant to assert this.[8]

Finally, some Polish-Americans revolted. Between 1897 and 1904 twenty-four parishes, claiming twenty thousand members, broke from the Church of Rome and created a Church uniquely their own, the Polish National Catholic Church. In 1912, a splinter Lithuanian National Catholic Church followed suit. After the revolt, Rome forced the Irish-American clergy to loosen their stranglehold on the Church in the United States. But by then it was too late. Most Polish-Americans remained within the Roman Catholic Church, but the Polish National Catholic Church continues as an independent church today.

Eastern Europeans had not come to America in order to discard their Old World values. They treasured them, and wanted their children to continue their traditions, honor their cultural heritage, and speak their language. In Mary Boreth's family for example:

My father hadn't learned much English because the Hungarians always spoke to each other in Hungarian. We children were not allowed to speak English in the house. And then on Saturdays we would go to the church school where we learned Hungarian reading and writing. I can do that even today fluently.[9]

The churches were the most important agency for transmitting the immigrants' cultures and beliefs to their American-raised children. Just as they did under foreign rule in Europe, the churches strove to preserve the culture and customs of their people. Practically every Polish parish had its own parochial school, which taught the Polish language, Polish history, and the obedience and morality that Polish parents expected of their children. In 1920, more than half of Polish-American children were attending Polish parochial schools. Even those who didn't were given cultural reinforcement in church-sponsored recreational activities, such as singing and orchestral groups, and literary and dramatic clubs.

In the peasant villages and Jewish ghettos of eastern Europe, the community had looked after the welfare of its members. Immigrants formed mutual aid societies in the United States to continue this tradition. The societies provided their members with health and life insurance, a circle of sympathetic countrypeople, and educational and recreational activities. Over time, local mutual aid organizations joined with others to form national societies, such as the National Croatian Society, whose statement of purpose was

to help people of Croatian race residing in America in cases of distress, sickness, and death, to educate and instruct them in the English language and in other studies to fit them for the duties of life and citizenship with our English-speaking people, to teach them and impress upon them the importance and duty of being naturalized under the laws of the United States.[10]

Immigrant associations sponsored charities to help the destitute, and credit unions to help the ambitious start businesses. They helped newly arrived immigrants find jobs and lodgings. They provided their members with a place to meet, in rented store-fronts, churches, and synagogues in the early days and later, as they grew more prosperous, in their own buildings. They assembled libraries and opened reading rooms where members could read native-language newspapers, from both the United States and Europe. Kenneth D. Miller described some of the activities of the early 1920s:

In almost every Slavic community one finds a Czech or Slovak or Polish or Croatian national hall, which is the headquarters of most of the national organizations. Many of these halls are large and imposing buildings. . . . There is a restaurant or saloon on the ground floor, from which much of the revenue for the up-keep of the hall is derived. . . . There one can secure Russian *borscht* (cabbage soup), and drink tea from a glass as in Moscow. The *knedlikv* (dumplings) so dear to the hearts of the Czechs . . . can be had, or *halushkv* (noodles in Slovak style).

Here also the leaders of the district congregate to discuss the political affairs of the old country or the politics of their group life in America. . . . Every such building has a large hall which serves both as a gymnasium and as an auditorium. And there are a number of smaller rooms for the societies' meetings and for educational work. On Saturday and Sunday mornings the children come for instruction in their mother tongue. On Saturday evenings there are dances and balls which last well into the morning. . . . On Sunday afternoons theatrical performances in the native tongue or concerts by native artists are given.[11]

The Falcons' Unions or sokols were also prominent activity centers in Slavic communities. These gymnastic societies, which had originated in Europe, put young men through a regimen of exercises and drills which aimed "to develop in [their] members, not only a sound body, but such qualities as courage, faithfulness to duty, and love of country."[12]

For a less structured, more relaxed social atmosphere, there were neighborhood taverns and cafés. These leisure haunts gave their neighborhoods a great deal of their Old Country flavor.

Taverns also provided other community services. Louis Adamic described the taverns he visited in the Pennsylvania coal and steel regions, as he swung through selling subscriptions for a Slovenian-American newspaper in 1916:

In 1891, the United States had passed a law excluding immigrants who showed symptoms of certain "loathsome or contagious diseases." Some immigrants who were turned back suffered from trachoma, which attacked the eyes and could lead to blindness. An old photo shows U.S. inspectors examining the eyes of immigrants on Ellis Island, 1907. (Courtesy of the Library of Congress.)

Eighty percent of the immigrants arriving in the United States landed in New York. Ellis Island, the immigrant station, was opened in 1892. Here immigrants could safely change money, buy train and boat tickets, and get information on lodgings. In this photo a throng of new arrivals makes its way through inspection in 1904. (Courtesy of the Library of Congress.)

An early view of Ellis Island and New York Harbor in 1891. By the time it closed in 1943, sixteen million immigrants had passed through it. (Courtesy of the Library of Congress.)

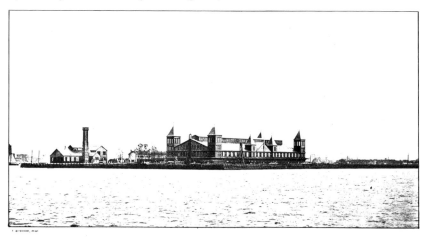

VIEW OF ELLIS ISLAND. NEW YORK HARBOR

Immigrant workers experienced all the ills of an industrial age largely unregulated by law or social conscience. In Pennsylvania, boys were apprenticed to the coal mines as early as the age of nine. Their careers began in the "breakers," picking out pieces of slate and other refuse from the coal on its way to the washers. Lewis Hine photographed the Ewen Breaker of the Pennsylvania Coal Co. in 1911. The dust was dense, and a slave driver stood ready to prod the boys. (National Archives.)

In New York City, children worked beside their immigrant parents in the tenement apartments that served as home and shop to many a family. Here a Jewish family and neighbors make garters until late at night. (Photo by Lewis Hine, 1912. National Archives.)

America was hard on eastern European immigrants. It offered them the worst jobs, the lowest wages, the most wretched living quarters. Here two officials of the New York City Tenement House Department inspect a cluttered basement living room, ca. 1900. (National Archives.)

The places where immigrants settled became communities where the immigrants reconstructed a familiar world. At the Hester Street Market on the Lower East Side in New York, ca. 1900, foods and goods were hawked from pushcarts and stands as they had been in the Old World village squares. (Courtesy of the Library of Congress.)

THE ONLY WAY TO HANDLE IT.

Immigrants were blamed for a host of social problems, including unemployment, poverty, crime, and Bolshevism, among others. In 1921, the first quota law restricted the number of immigrants of each nationality admitted to the United States each year to three percent of the foreign born of that nationality living in the United States in 1910. In this cartoon by Hallahan, which appeared in the *Literary Digest* in 1921, Uncle Sam cuts off immigration. (Courtesy of the Library of Congress.)

In some years, the number of eastern Europeans leaving the United States to return home equaled half the number of those coming into the country. "Birds of passage" they were called: those staying in America only a few years. But many didn't return home at all—either because they hadn't the money or because they got used to life in the United States and found it hard to backtrack. Some were able to make visits home to tell about their new lives, such as this man, who returned briefly to his native village in the western Ukraine in 1929. (Courtesy of Olga Litowinsky.)

Immigrants continued to arrive in the United States escaping events in Europe, such as the Bolshevik revolution in 1917 and its subsequent turmoil, and the coming to power of Hitler in Germany in the 1930s. During World War II, many immigrants supported the American war effort. The following group of photographs shows the variety of people and nationalities who contributed so much to life in their new country:

Bohemian farmers in the cutover land area near Black River Falls, Wisconsin. (Photo by Russell Lee, 1937. Courtesy of the Library of Congress.)

An Estonian farm family in Connecticut. (Photo by Jim Collier, 1942. Courtesy of the Library of Congress.)

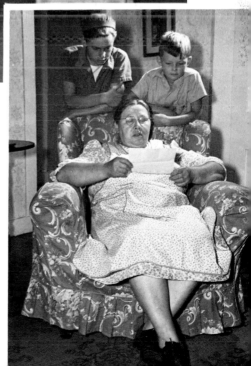

An immigrant farmer and rabbi (with the Torah) in Connecticut. (Photo by John Collier, 1942. Courtesy of the Library of Congress.)

A Polish farmer's wife in Connecticut reading aloud a letter from her son in the United States armed forces. (Photo by John Collier, 1942. Courtesy of the Library of Congress.)

Many immigrants chose heavy industry over farm life. They lived in such steel towns as Midland, Pennsylvania, shown here in 1941. (Photo by Jack Delano. Courtesy of the Library of Congress.)

A Croatian steelworker stops by the hall of the Steel Workers Organizing Committee in Midland (1941). (Photo by Jack Delano. Courtesy of the Library of Congress.)

Russian steelworkers on their way to work in Midland (1941). (Photo by Jack Delano. Courtesy of the Library of Congress.)

Six million Jews did not survive World War II. They were victims of Hitler's hatred and his attempt at genocide. In May 1945, Allied liberating armies found appalling atrocities. In Nuremberg, Germany, the Americans came upon a mass murder of Polish Jews by SS troops and ordered townspeople to provide coffins and pallbearers and to attend a service in a cemetery. (U.P.I.)

This elderly Polish couple arrived in New York in 1947 for a reunion with a son and daughter living there. They came from Siberia, where they had been sent with other refugees after fleeing eastward before the Nazi invasion of Poland. Two daughters were killed in the invasion. (U.P.I.)

After Soviet tanks and troops put down the Hungarian revolution in 1956, thousands fled across the border into Austria. The family at left has made its way across fields and through woods. They and the others behind them have brought with them only what they can carry. Some thirty thousand were admitted to the United States through special legislation. (U.P.I.)

The millionth European to be moved to a new home after eight years of international migration sponsorship arrived in New York in 1960. Born in a Displaced Persons Camp, this young boy is the son of a Latvian couple who fled from the Russians. (U.P.I.)

The churches strove to preserve the culture and customs of their people. In 1978, Polish-Americans in Chicago, the city with the largest population of Polish people outside of Warsaw, rejoiced at the news that a Polish cardinal had been elected pope. Here neighborhood children look at a photograph of John Paul II. (U.P.I.)

The saloon was no mere drinking-place, but a . . . boarding-house equipped to cater to a great many needs of the colony. There one could not only drown one's sorrows, overcome one's weariness from long and hard toil, and meet one's fellows; one could also buy steamship tickets and money-orders for folks in the Old Country, play poker, eat, dance, have one's letters written, enjoy a girl, subscribe to newspapers, pay one's lodge and club dues, and—if the saloon-keeper was on friendly terms with the priest, which was not unusual even one's church dues!

The saloon-keeper . . . was a jolly fellow who knew all the members of the colony by their first names, had a glad hand for the humblest workingman, and if the latter got into trouble with the police, intervened on his behalf. The unmarried men with no permanent addresses received their mail addressed in his care. Usually he was a notary public. . . . Sometimes he acted as matrimonial agent, and wedding festivities usually were held in the hall above his saloon.[13]

A *New York Tribune* reporter described the Lower East Side's Russian-Jewish cafés in 1900:

These people want no saloons. When they drink liquor, they drink at home. . . . But their tea, they take in public and over it discuss the questions of the day for hours at a time. In these cafes there is much political work done, much earnest and clever talk on the problems of government. . . .

At most hours of the day and night, until three o'clock in the morning, these places are filled with men who have come there to sip Russian tea out of tumblers, meet their friends, and discuss everything under heaven. They are the intellectual aristocracy of the East Side, though aristocracy is a word tabooed among them. . . .

The literary men, the newspaper writers, the actors, the professional men form the clientele of the cafes. . . . Nearly all are of radical opinions. The air of the East Side is unfavorable to conservatism. Too much is remembered of the old Russian home across the water, and . . . the habit of being "ag'in the government," once formed, is not easily broken.[14]

Marcus Ravage described going to lecture programs with his friends on the Lower East Side:

There were scores of lectures every week. . . . One night it was Darwin, and the next it might be the principles of air-pressure. On a Saturday night there were sometimes two meetings so arranged that both could be attended by the same audience. I remember going once to a meeting at Cooper Union to protest against the use of the militia in breaking a strike somewhere in the West, and then retiring with a crowd of others to . . . an informal discussion on "Hamlet *versus* Don Quixote." It did not matter to us what the subject was. . . . Our poor, cramped souls were yearning to be inspired and uplifted.[15]

The most popular entertainment was the Yiddish theater. Whether farce or melodrama, the plays were grounded in daily life in the ghetto, offering the audiences something that every social and intellectual class could relate to. Hutchins Hapgood, an American journalist who was an enthusiastic observer of the Jewish neighborhood, described its theater audiences:

Into these . . . buildings crowd the Jews of all the Ghetto classes—the sweat-shop woman with her baby, the day-laborer, the small Hester Street shopkeeper, the Russian-Jewish anarchist and socialist, the Ghetto rabbi and scholar, the poet, the journalist. The poor and ignorant are in the great majority, but the learned, the intellectual and the progressive are also represented. . . . The socialists and the literati create the demand that forces into the mass of vaudeville, light opera, historical and melodramatic plays a more serious art element. . . . But this more serious element is so saturated with the simple manners, humor and pathos of the life of the poor Jew, that it is seldom above the heartfelt understanding of the crowd.[16]

Another major cultural force in every immigrant community was the native language press. Daily, weekly, and monthly journals kept immigrants informed of events in the Old Country, and helped them understand the events that touched their lives in the new. In their heyday, there were sixty Polish-language newspapers published in the United States. In 1920, there were four Czech dailies in Chicago alone.

The most famous and influential of the immigrant newspapers was the *Jewish Daily Forward,* which is still published in New York today. Abraham Cahan, its editor for its first fifty years, felt that the purpose of the paper was to interpret America to the immigrants. This he did in his editorials, and in the famous *"Bintl Brief"* (Bundle of Letters) column. Readers wrote for advice on every aspect of life. Here is a small sampling:

1906

Dear Editor,

I am a Russian revolutionist and a freethinker. Here in America I became acquainted with a girl who is also a freethinker. We decided to marry, but the problem is that she has Orthodox parents, and for their sake we must have a religious ceremony. . . . Her parents also want me to go to the synagogue with them before the wedding, and I don't know what to do. Therefore I ask you to advise me how to act.

ANSWER:
The advice is that there are times when it pays to give in to old parents and not to grieve them. . . .

1907

Worthy Editor,

. . . There are seven people in our family—parents and five children. I am the oldest child, a fourteen-year-old girl. We have been in the country two years and my father, who is a frail man, is the only one working to support the whole family.

I go to school, where I do very well. But since times are hard now and my father earned only five dollars this week, I began to talk about giving up my studies and going to work in order to help father as much as possible. But my mother didn't even want to hear of it. She wants me to continue my education. . . .

I have a lot of compassion for my parents. My mother is now pregnant, but she still has to take care of the three boarders we have in the house.

. . . I beg you to tell me how to act. . . .

ANSWER:
The advice to the girl is that she should obey her parents and further her education because in that way she will be able to give them

greater satisfaction than if she went out to
work.

1908

Dear Editor,

. . . I am a young man of twenty-five, sixteen
years in America, and recently met a fine girl.
She has a flaw, however, that keeps me from
marrying her. The fault is that she has a
dimple in her chin, and it is said that people
who have this lose their first husband or
wife. . . .

ANSWER:

The tragedy is not that the girl has a dimple in
her chin but that some people have a screw
loose in their heads! . . . It's truly shameful
that a young man who was brought up in
America should ask such a question.[17]

The old ways and the new clashed in every immigrant community. How much to change? How
"Americanized" to become? At one extreme, immigrants, if they chose, could live in their ethnic
neighborhoods as if they were the Old World trans-
planted. Stoyan Christowe remarked:

Many had been in America for ten years and
still they were strangers in this country. They
lived in special worlds which they had created
for themselves in America, little worlds
fashioned somewhat after their own old-

country worlds. . . . They thought old-country thoughts, spoke only their native tongues, were interested in the political and nationalist movements of their own peoples and were insulated from the world that surrounded them. They were impervious to the currents, political, social, economic, cultural, about them. They sat in their coffeehouses sipping Turkish coffee and playing cards and backgammon and talking old-country politics.[18]

For many immigrants it was hard to become "Americanized." Work and the struggle to survive took the greatest part of their energies. Coming from the narrow worlds of the peasant village and the Jewish ghetto, they were not prepared to plunge into life outside their close-knit communities. Other Americans were often not helpful—they mocked the immigrants' languages and manners; they called them rude names. A 1920 study in New Jersey listed an array of reasons why immigrants surveyed chose not to attend night school classes in English and in American cultural and academic subjects.

The following are some of the reasons given by the men and women themselves, Poles, Russians, Hungarians, Bohemians, . . . as to why they did not attend evening school:

How can I? I work at night.

I work now during the day, but my wife works at night and I have to stay at home to take care of the children. . . .

It is childish. We keep saying all the time, "This is a desk"; "This is a door." I know it is a desk and a door. What for keep saying it all the time?

My teacher, she was very nice young lady, but very young. She does not understand what I want to talk about or know about.

7:30 P.M. to 9:30 P.M. is too long; you get home too late. . . . It is 10:30 before you get to bed and that is too late for a spinner.

They treat you like a child because you don't know English.

Too tired.[19]

Nevertheless, through work, immigrants were forced into contact with American values. Through school, immigrants' children learned English and studied American culture and history. They even learned that America was a "melting pot"! In play-grounds, candy stores, and city streets, they were introduced to the culture of other immigrant groups and of American society at large. Songs, books, movies, advertisements—and as the children grew up, career ambitions—all served to woo them from the world of their parents.

Nowhere was this more apparent than among Jews. It was nearly impossible to perform all the religious observances required of Jews while work-ing in the shops and factories of the United States. Employers did not allow Jews time for their daily periods of prayer, and for their Sabbath and many holy days. The intellectual and political pursuits of many immigrant Jews were another sign of change. In the Old World, they had been allowed little but the religious life; in the United States, many other choices were open. The great majority of American-raised children fell away from Orthodox religious observance. Some joined Conservative or Reform congregations, the versions of the religion that evolved in America and allowed looser interpretations of the ancient laws. Some abandoned religious observance altogether. Religion had flourished where it was persecuted, and lost its hold on the people in a climate of religious freedom.

With their American educations, the children of the immigrants moved away from the blue-collar world of their parents into offices, commerce, and even professions. In doing so, they were exposed to a different way of life. A 1905 article in the *Jewish Daily Forward* explored the careers pursued by the daughters of the immigrant garment workers:

> They become salesladies or typists. . . . Salaries for typists are very low—some work for as little as three dollars a week. . . . But typists have more [status] than shopgirls; . . . they come in contact with a more refined class of people.
> Typists therefore live in two different worlds: they work in a sunny, spacious office,

they speak and hear only English, their
superiors call them "Miss." And then they
come home to dirty rooms and to parents who
aren't always so courteous.[20]

An unhappy parent wrote the following letter to the
Jewish Daily Forward in 1938:

I am a man in my fifties, and I came to
America when I was very young. I don't have
to tell you how hard life was for a "greenhorn"
in those times. I suffered plenty. But that didn't
keep me from falling in love with a girl from
my home town and marrying her. . . .

The years flew fast and before we looked
around we were parents of four children who
brightened and sweetened our lives.

The children were dear and smart and we
gave them an education that was more than we
could afford. They went to college, became
professionals, and are well established.

Suddenly I feel as if the floor has collapsed
under my feet. I don't know how to express it,
but the fact that my children are well educated
and have outgrown me makes me feel bad. I
can't talk to them about my problems and they
can't talk to me about theirs. It's as if there
were a deep abyss that divides us.

. . . I often think it might be better for me
if they were not so well educated, but ordinary
workingmen, like me. Then we would have
more in common.[21]

But the Old World ties don't die easy, and many a fourth-generation American today still speaks of him- or herself as a Polish-American, a Hungarian-American, or one of the other varieties of eastern European Americans. American Jews still celebrate Jewish music, literature, and history, even if they no longer keep the faith.

After World War I, Poles, Czechs, and Slovaks in the United States helped persuade the American government to support the rebirth of their homelands as independent nations. Their descendants still take a close interest in the affairs of eastern Europe today, as American Jews do in the affairs of Israel. Churches and national societies still teach the Old World languages to those who want to learn them, and keep alive the songs, dances, and folklore of the Old Countries. Yiddish, which had been regarded as a dead language after the Nazi annihilation of eastern European Jews, is being studied again today on several American campuses. In 1978, a writer born in Poland, living in New York, and writing in Yiddish, Isaac Bashevis Singer, was awarded the Nobel Prize for Literature. Could this only have happened in America? Very probably so, for here this writer could find his audience. And when the Polish Pope John Paul II visited the United States in 1979, it was very clear that descendants of Polish immigrants considered him one of their own.

Immigrants banded together in ethnic communities because they were vulnerable, strangers in the land, confused, abused, and exploited. They derived strength and support from each other. Louis Adamic summarized this well:

> The more pronounced the difference in language, ways, and conditions in America and in the immigrant's own country, the more urgent it was for him to seek out his country-men.[22]

Time and experience in America changed the ways in which the immigrants and their children lived. But parts of the Old World cultures survived to enrich and change American life. The immigrants' legacies weren't just foods, music, religious beliefs, and community organizations. Irving Howe, a historian of the Jewish immigration from eastern Europe, expressed perhaps the most important contribution the immigrants made to the American "pot":

> We cannot be our fathers, we cannot live like our mothers, but we may look to their experience for images of rectitude and purities of devotion. . . . They thrust before us the most fundamental questions of human existence: how shall we live? What are the norms by which we can make judgments of the "good life"? Which modes of conduct may enable us to establish a genuine community?[23]

Chapter 8

The Labor Wars

In Virginia, Governor Sir George Yeardley issued the call for an assembly meeting in the Jamestown church on July 30, 1619, to organize the first representative legislative assembly in America. . . . All native-born Englishmen were allowed to vote; all foreign-born Virginians were excluded.

The Polish settlers and their families, who felt they had contributed quite enough to the survival of the colony, demanded a right to vote and, when the governor refused it, staged the first strike . . . in America. . . .

They said: no vote, no work.[1]

W. S. KUNICZAK

That first strike in Virginia—which, by the way, got the Poles the rights that they wanted—was a forecast of things to come. Some three centuries later, eastern European immigrants again staged strikes, this time to establish labor unions in American industries.

Labor unions were not widely established in the United States until the late 1930s. It took many battles in many industries to accomplish this, too many to cover here. This chapter will focus on two dramatic episodes in the labor wars near the turn of the century: a spontaneous strike of Slavic workers in the anthracite coal fields of eastern Pennsylvania; and a pair of strikes by Jewish workers in the garment factories of New York. These two campaigns describe how eastern European workers changed the labor movement, and how the labor movement changed them.

On August 12, 1897, Gomer Jones, mining superintendent of the Lehigh and Wilkes-Barre Company, posted a new work rule which stated that mule drivers, who were almost all eastern European or Italian immigrants, would be required to work additional hours, but with no additional pay. Jones was a tough boss:

> When I came here a year ago, I came to restore discipline in the mines and to operate them [profitably]. The discipline was . . . lax. The men did about as they pleased. The two superintendents here then associated with the men, mixed with them, drank with them and were regarded as "hail fellows well met." . . .

Now I cannot do that. . . . I've never made
it a practice to hobnob with the men. . . .
When I give orders I expect them to be
obeyed. . . . I dismissed a good many men—
about 80, I think.[2]

The new work rule struck the mule drivers as one
oppressive rule too many. They stopped work.
Jones tried to force them back to work, with the
aid of a club. The mine workers beat him off.

The discontent spread. Immigrant workers at
other mines had grievances, too, most of them con-
cerning their low pay. The next day, three thousand
workers stayed out, and forced six mines to close.
A local newsman toured several Slavic neighborhoods and reported:

Never in all our experience have we met a
more determined body of strikers.[3]

By September, five thousand immigrant laborers
were on strike. They marched through the coal
towns, shouting their anger, brandishing fence posts
and American flags. On September 2, the *Wilkes-
Barre Times* expressed the alarm of the English-
speaking community at the immigrants' action:

Thousands of ignorant foreigners have begun
a reign of terror, have closed up all the
collieries, wrecked the home of the superintendent [Jones], and marched from one mine
to another amid the wildest confusion, a
howling mob without aim or leader.[4]

The other inhabitants of the coal towns, many of them immigrants themselves from the British Isles, regarded the eastern and southern Europeans as ignorant, dirty, and violent.

The majority of the strikers were eastern Europeans—Poles, Lithuanians, Slovaks, and Ukrainians. Despite the lack of outside support, the strikers demanded that their communities maintain a solid front. "Round-up squads" attacked the Slavic mine workers who did not join their demonstrations.

At a house on the outskirts of McAdoo, a Hun* too tired to march sought seclusion in the cellar of his house. But the keen scent of the round-up squad ferreted him out and he was assisted into the line on the end of eight clubs applied to his person in none too gently a manner. The scene was too affecting for his wife; she was assisted to her front yard and consoled by her sympathetic neighbors. There [were] many of these scenes along the line of march.[5]

Local newspapers described the strikers' progress as if they were covering a war. It *was* a war to the strikers. They were fighting for a living wage against

* A derogatory term derived from "Hungarian," but applied haphazardly to all eastern Europeans. There was only a small Magyar population in the coal towns at this time. Most of those who were called "Huns" were actually Slovaks.

an enemy determined to keep them down. They stormed the coal breakers at the entrances to the still-working mines, and drove off the still-working miners.

> The column moved on to Jeansville where a halt was called. . . . Then with a cheer the army descended on No. 1 breaker. Down through the strippings, over culm banks, through groves and over fields came the army of strikers like an avalanche.
>
> Hark! the deep-toned whistle of the breaker announced the onslaught . . . and warned the working miners to defend themselves which they did by chasing out of the breaker and doing a hundred-yard dash over the adjacent hills. Hurrah! The breaker was won without a struggle, the enemy had fled.[6]

Day after day the immigrants marched and demonstrated. Their fury frightened the English-speaking community. Public pressure persuaded the sheriffs of the counties involved to raise posses to break up the marches. Then the real violence came.

On September 10, a group of Poles, Lithuanians, and Slovaks marched to the town of Lattimer to shut down a mine. They were met by a sheriff and an armed posse. The sheriff ordered them off. In the confusion, the sheriff went down. Whether he fell or was pushed was never made clear.

The sheriff ordered his men to shoot into the crowd of unarmed demonstrators. Nineteen demonstrators were killed, and thirty-nine wounded. Most were shot in the back as they fled.

After what became known as the "Lattimer Massacre," the strike of the immigrant mine workers was no longer just local news. The deaths were reported around the country and the world, and stirred up a storm of outrage. The Slavic-American press demanded that the "murderers" be punished. (The sheriff and sixty-seven members of the posse later stood trial, but all were found not guilty.) Polish-, Lithuanian-, and Russian-American societies contributed funds to assist the strikers. The Austro-Hungarian government demanded—unsuccessfully—that the victims' families be compensated.

The mine owners could no longer stand firm in the face of the public outcry. All but one of the companies buckled and offered the strikers some improvements in pay and working conditions. Ten days after the killings, miners were returning to work.

But the war wasn't quite over. Some immigrant factions wanted to hold out for greater gains, and now a dramatic new force joined them in battle. "Big Mary" Septek, a Polish boardinghouse keeper, led a brigade of women armed with clubs, rolling pins, and pokers in attacks on workers who had returned to their jobs. The *Wilkes-Barre Record* commented:

The appearance of women as a factor in a coal region strike is a novelty of a not very pleasing nature. Those who have made themselves so conspicuous the past week . . . were the wives, mothers, and sisters of the Hungarian, Polish and Italian strikers, and it is assumed that they had the sanction of their husbands, sons, and brothers in their ill-advised demonstrations.

. . . Such scenes would have been impossible in the troubles between capital and labor . . . when our mines were manned by English-speaking men. . . . This . . . is only another . . . forcible illustration of the great change that has taken place in these coal regions since the importation of cheap European labor commenced.[7]

In any case, the women's action came too late to have much effect. The strike had run out of steam. Most of the men felt that the settlements the owners offered were all they could realistically expect. By October 4, almost two months after the strike began, all the mines were working again.

On the surface, the strikers had not accomplished much. Gomer Jones's work rule was rescinded. There were small increases in pay and slight improvements in working conditions. But no union had been involved. No collective bargaining rights had been sought or won. The improvements wrung from the mine owners could easily, at the owners' whim, be revoked.

Under the surface, though, the revolt of the immigrant mine workers laid the groundwork for future union victories. Until the 1890s, no union had been able to get started in the anthracite region, although several attempts had been made. Mine owners refused to deal with unions. Early unions lacked the organization, the discipline, and the funds to keep workers out on long strikes.

In 1894, the United Mine Workers of America (UMW), which had organized bituminous coal mine workers in western Pennsylvania, Ohio, and Illinois, sent organizers to the anthracite fields in eastern Pennsylvania. For a time, they had some success. Several thousand workers enrolled. Eastern Europeans were particularly enthusiastic, for the organizers had made special efforts to enlist them.

In the past, group prejudices had divided the work force and had stood in the way of effective organization. The veteran, more skilled miners resented the eastern European influx. They felt that the flood of cheap immigrant labor brought down the wages of all mine workers. They also were contemptuous of the languages and customs of the newcomers.

But, by the turn of the century, eastern Europeans constituted about fifty percent of the work force. They were too numerous for UMW leaders to ignore. So they employed Slavic organizers to address rallies in the Slavic languages. They appointed eastern Europeans as district officers. They published their *Journal* in several languages. And eastern Europeans responded by joining the union in greater numbers than English-speaking miners.

Then, in 1896, the union drive came to a halt. The main problem, simply, was that the union didn't have the funds to continue. Workers attended rallies, but given their low wages, most were reluctant to pay dues to an untried organization. Union organizers left the region, and union locals disbanded.

The immigrants' revolt in 1897 changed all this. The strikers asked the union organizers to return to the anthracite region, and the union men rushed back, for now there was a truly aroused work force there. A month after the strike ended, sixty-four UMW locals had been established.

In 1900 and 1902, the UMW led two strikes that resulted in the establishment of collective bargaining in the anthracite industry. It took the union thirteen more years to win complete union recognition from the owners, but the union was well on its way, entrenched in the region. This was one of labor's great early victories.

In 1902, the UMW strike lasted five months, yet the ill-paid immigrants were not starved into surrender. Eastern European immigrants were obsessed with thrift and savings. Every land-hungry peasant who had been starved out of eastern Europe still dreamed of owning land, for land meant security and prosperity. So despite their low wages, the immigrants managed, through strict economy, to save money. Almost every family took in boarders, which kept down living expenses for landlord and lodger alike. Households kept their food costs low

—bread and potatoes were their staples. When it came to a strike, the money they had put away and their thrifty habits enabled them to hold out longer and better than any other workers in the coal towns. And because they formed so large a part of the work force, their endurance made a difference.

The future success of the UMW was assured by the 1897 strike action. But there was an immediate gain that was equally important. Mine owners and supervisors had regarded the immigrant workers as little more than beasts of burden on whom they could make outrageous demands and to whom they could pay next to nothing. After 1897, they could no longer treat this work force as less than human, at least not without fear of reprisal. Gomer Jones's rule had unleashed a terrible fury. It changed the way the immigrants regarded themselves and the way they dealt with others. As an 1897 newspaper commented:

> Gomer had learned a lesson. He has been taught a man is a man even if he is a Hungarian.[8]

On November 22, 1909, a spillover crowd of shirt-waist makers packed the auditorium of Cooper Union, a working-class college on the fringe of the Lower East Side in New York. They were almost all women, two-thirds of them Jewish, most of the rest Italian, and almost all in their teens and early twenties. They had come to decide whether to call a general strike in the city's shirtwaist, or women's blouse, industry.

Local 25, the shirtwaist makers' local, of the International Ladies' Garment Workers Union (ILGWU) had staged the rally. Founded in 1900, it had thus far made little progress in organizing the garment trades. In November 1909, the shirtwaist makers' local could count only about one hundred members, and had just four dollars in its treasury.

A limited strike had been going on since September against two manufacturers, the Leiserson Company and the Triangle Waist Company. But these actions were on the verge of collapse. Strike-breakers and thugs hired by the employers were weakening the strikers' resolve.

The union was at a turning point. Could it become a force in the garment industry, or would it wither away like earlier unions that had failed to dent the manufacturers' resistance?

Eminent labor leaders addressed the rally, including Samuel Gompers, president of the AFL. But the leaders seemed reluctant to bring the issue to a vote. They were unsure of the strength and determination of the ILGWU and the young workers.

Suddenly teen-ager Clara Lemlich, who had been picketing the Leiserson Company daily, ran up to the platform. She cried out passionately in Yiddish:

> I am a working girl, one of those striking against intolerable conditions. I am tired of

listening to speakers who talk in generalities. What we are here for is to decide whether or not to strike. I offer a resolution that a general strike be declared—now.

The women shouted their agreement. The chairman of the meeting called for order and asked:

Do you mean it in good faith? Will you take the Jewish oath?

The women raised their hands and solemnly spoke the ancient words:

If I turn traitor to the cause I now pledge, may this hand wither from the arm I raise![9]

Twenty thousand women went on strike. They had good cause. Employers believed that because most of them hoped to marry and escape the factories, and because women were generally thought to be less assertive than men, they would not protest being exploited. They earned as little as three dollars a week in some cases. They had to pay for the needles and electrical power they used, for the chairs they sat on, and the lockers where they hung their coats. They were fined if they came to work five minutes late.

The strike galvanized the immigrant community. These, after all, were their daughters, and the picket lines stood only blocks from their homes. The Jewish press urged the strikers' cause, and veteran unionists counseled the strike leaders.

Help came from outside the community as well. Social workers and investigative journalists publicized the strikers' complaints and helped enlist public sympathy. Society women contributed to the bail fund, and prominent attorneys defended arrested pickets for free. Women's groups were particularly supportive. Women's colleges contributed to the strike funds, and female students walked the picket lines with their working-class sisters. The Women's Trade Union League and the National Women's Suffrage Association (for American women were still a decade away from having the right to vote) held sympathy meetings. The labor lawyer Morris Hillquit commented:

> It is no mere accident that in this fight the striking Jewish and Italian girls, the poorest of the poor, have the sympathy and active support of the suffrage workers of all classes. There is a certain common bond between women fighting for civil rights and women fighting for industrial justice.[10]

All New York was singing the tune, "Heaven Will Protect the Working Girl."

But there were some who disagreed that Heaven was on the women's side. Sentencing a striker, a New York judge lectured her:

> You are on strike against God and Nature, whose firm law is that man shall earn the bread in the sweat of his brow.[11]

The forces of law had allied with the employers to scare the women into backing down. In the first month of the strike, 723 women were arrested, and 19 were sent to the workhouse. Police offered little aid as thugs herding strikebreakers through the picket lines attacked the striking workers. McAlister Coleman, who was a young reporter in 1909, years later recalled an attack that he witnessed:

> The girls, headed by teen-age Clara Lemlich, described by union organizers as a "pint of trouble for the bosses," began singing Italian and Russian working-class songs as they paced in twos before the factory door. Of a sudden, around the corner came a dozen tough-looking customers, for whom the union label "gorillas" seemed well-chosen.
>
> "Stand fast, girls," called Clara, and then the thugs rushed the line, knocking Clara to her knees, striking at the pickets, opening the way for a group of frightened scabs to slip through the broken line. . . . There was a confused melee of scratching, screaming girls and fist-swinging men and then a patrol wagon arrived. The thugs ran off as the cops pushed Clara and two other badly beaten girls into the wagon.

Coleman caught a glimpse that day of an America he had never known.

I followed the rest of the retreating pickets to the union hall, a few blocks away. There a relief station had been set up where one bottle of milk and a loaf of bread were given to strikers with small children in their families. There, for the first time in my comfortably sheltered, upper West Side life, I saw real hunger on the faces of my fellow Americans in the richest city in the world.[12]

The strike lasted five months, until mid-February 1910. It was finally settled with some improvements in working conditions, and membership in Local 25 had increased one hundred times, to over ten thousand. But the strike had failed to force the manufacturers to recognize the union, and had not created a lasting machinery to handle future workers' grievances.

Some of this came, though, within the year. Five months after the strike of "our wonderful fervent girls,"[13] as one old trade union hand called them, seventy thousand men who worked in women's coat and cloak factories called their general strike. Abraham Rosenberg, president of the ILGWU, recalled the emotions of the strike leaders as they watched the men pour out of the factories into the streets, on the first day of the strike:

We saw a sea of people surging out of the side streets toward Fifth Avenue. . . . By half past two, all the streets were jammed with

thousands of workers. . . . Many of our most
devoted members cried for joy at the idea
that their lifelong labors had been crowned
with success. In my mind I could only picture
to myself such a scene taking place when the
Jews were led out of Egypt.[14]

The cloakmakers had three demands: better wages,
better hours, and union recognition. The employers
were willing to negotiate on the first two issues.
They refused to deal with the last.

The owners, like most of the strikers, were
Jewish, and the conflict was tearing the community
apart. Finally, a group of prominent Jewish busi-
nessmen proposed that a Boston attorney, Louis D.
Brandeis (who would later become a Supreme
Court justice), arbitrate the strike.

Brandeis's strike settlement was a milestone in
labor history. He persuaded the manufacturers to
accept "preferential union shops," or shops in which
union members would be hired before nonunion
workers. He persuaded them to allow a Board of
Arbitration and a Board of Grievances to handle
future disputes between workers and employers.
Brandeis's settlement wasn't quite union recognition,
but it advanced the union cause considerably.

Between September 1909 and September 1910,
Jewish garment workers had successfully waged
two major collective actions. Like the Slavic mine
workers, the Jewish garment workers mobilized
their community to support the workers' cause.

Where the Slavs drew strength from their communal village traditions, the Jews drew inspiration from their religious traditions. Even the manufacturers were to some extent swayed by the force of Jewish ethical law. Like the Pennsylvanians, the New Yorkers achieved one of American labor's significant early victories, and made their union a force in their industry. And like their fellow eastern Europeans, they transformed themselves into a community that insisted on its rights and its dignity. The Yiddish poet Abraham Liessen summed up the change:

> The 70,000 zeros [in the cloak factories] became 70,000 fighters.[15]

Six months after the cloakmakers' settlement, tragedy struck. On March 26, 1911, fire erupted in the Triangle Waist Company, one of the first companies struck by "the fervent girls," and the largest shirtwaist factory in the city. Eight hundred and fifty employees worked there behind locked doors. Within ten minutes, 146 of them, mostly Jewish and Italian women, were dead, and many more were left scarred physically and emotionally. The *New York World* reported the holocaust:

> The fire began in the eighth story. The flames licked and shot their way up through the other two stories. All three floors were occupied by the Triangle Waist Company. . . . The first signs that persons in the street knew that these

three top stories had turned into red furnaces in which human creatures were being caught and incinerated was when screaming men and women and boys and girls crowded out on the many window ledges and threw themselves into the streets far below. They jumped with their clothing ablaze. The hair of some of the girls streamed up aflame as they leaped. Thud after thud sounded on the pavements. . . . On both the Greene Street and Washington Place sides of the building there grew mounds of the dead and dying. . . .

Within the three flaming floors it was as frightful. . . . When Fire Chief Croker could make his way into these three floors, he found sights that utterly staggered him, that sent him, a man used to viewing horrors, back and down into the street with quivering lips. The floors were black with smoke. And then he saw as the smoke drifted away bodies burned to bare bones. There were skeletons bending over sewing machines.[16]

The factory, like many garment workshops, had been a firetrap. The labor activist Rose Schneiderman spoke at one of the many memorial meetings held for the dead women:

This is not the first time girls have been burned alive in this city. Every week I must learn of the untimely death of one of my sister workers. Every year thousands of us are maimed. The

life of men and women is so cheap and
property is so sacred! . . .
Too much blood has been spilled. . . . It is
up to the working people to save themselves.[17]

The Triangle fire and the Lattimer Massacre were
dramatic instances of the perils immigrants faced
both in their daily work lives and in their efforts to
improve their state. These tragedies tore the heart
out of the immigrant communities. But they also
strengthened the communities' resolve to fight for
change.

Eastern European immigrants fought in many
industries. In time, they succeeded. Along with the
UMW and the ILGWU, such important unions
today as the United Automobile Workers, the
United Steelworkers, and the Amalgamated Meat
Cutters and Butcher Workmen testify to the courage
and determination of immigrant workers in the first
third of this century. It is ironic that at the very
same period, the feelings of many Americans were
turning against the immigrants.

Chapter 9

The Gates Close

There is an appalling danger to the American wage earner from the flood of low, unskilled, ignorant, foreign labor which has poured into the country for some years past, and which not only takes lower wages, but accepts a standard of life and living so low that the American workingman cannot compete with it.[1]

SENATOR HENRY CABOT LODGE

At the end of the nineteenth century, Americans were debating whether to continue to allow an unrestricted flow of immigrants to enter the country. This was not the first time this issue had come up in American history. But this time was different: this time the restrictionists would have their way. By 1929, the United States had instituted a quota system which barred immigration from Asia and reduced the great tide that had been coming from eastern and southern Europe to barely a trickle.

Americans were reacting to what they considered two alarming turns of events. One was a great increase in the number of immigrants coming to the United States in the decades after the Civil War. And the other was a shift in the immigrants' places of origin from northern and western Europe to the less developed countries to the south and the east.

Statistics tell the tale: in the peak decade of immigration before the Civil War, 1851 to 1860, some two and a half million came from Europe. Only twenty-one thousand, or less than one percent, came from southern and eastern lands. After the war, the total numbers, and the percentages from Italy, Greece, the Balkans, Austro-Hungary, and the Russian Empire, kept spiraling up. Nearly five million Europeans came between 1871 and 1880; almost one million of them, or 20 percent, were from the south and the east. In the all-time peak decade of immigration, 1901 to 1910, over eight million Europeans arrived. Six million, or 75 percent of them, were from southern and eastern regions.

This meant, as we have seen, a great influx of the poor, the uneducated, the industrially unskilled. It meant the presence of foreign languages, strange customs, and suspect religions in an English-speaking, largely Protestant society.

As haystacks gave way to smokestacks on the

horizon, the immigrants who labored in mills and mines and dwelled in eye-sore urban and industrial slums, became for many Americans the symbols of the changes. This new, grimy, bustling, multicultural America made many older Americans uncomfortable.

They blamed immigrants for a host of social problems. In 1925, Kenneth D. Miller catalogued some of the charges:

> They have been held responsible for unemployment, child labor, lack of organization among wage-earners, strikes, radicalism and Bolshevism, congestion, poverty, crime, insanity, . . . parochial schools, atheism, political corruption, and municipal misrule.[2]

Few Americans cared that one charge often contradicted another. Few understood, as Miller did, that immigrants were not so much the causes of the problems as the victims.

> [The immigrant] did not make his own bed here in America, but found it made for him by our industrial system. . . . Our "immigrant problem" is but a phase of a serious industrial problem.[3]

Native-born workers, and workers who had immigrated here earlier, were among the most vocal critics of the new immigration. The Junior Order of American Mechanics said:

Will we American citizens allow the riff-raff of Europe, who will work for a matter of nothing and live on the refuse of the cess-pool and the garbage dump, to replace American labor and take our earnings back to foreign lands, to assist more filth and vice to land on our shores?[4]

Behind these economic arguments and social slurs lay a new fear. The historian John Higham identified it:

At the deepest level, what impelled the restriction movement . . . was the discovery that immigration was undermining the unity of American culture and threatening the accustomed dominance of a white Protestant people of northern European descent.[5]

Older Americans labeled the newcomers inferior peoples, unfit to wear the title "Americans." A new pseudoscience cropped up: a school of anthropology that classified white Europeans into three distinct "races." The most advanced race was said to be the Nordics—the English, Scots, Germans, and Scandinavians, with a few French Protestants thrown in. This was the race, it was held, from which the American people had sprung. These, it was said, were liberty-loving people of initiative; the other two races were the Mediterraneans of southern Europe and the Alpines of eastern Europe, less intelligent, less capable than the Nordics.

Madison Grant, the most influential of the racial theorists, wrote in his 1916 book, *The Passing of the Great Race*:

> The new immigration . . . contained a large and increasing number of the weak, the broken and mentally crippled of all races drawn from the lowest stratum of the Mediterranean basin and the Balkans, together with hordes of the wretched submerged populations of the Polish Ghettos. Our jails, insane asylums and alms-houses are filled with this human flotsam and the whole tone of American life, social, moral, and political, has been lowered and vulgarized by them.[6]

Racism had long been a fact of life in America. It had shaped the discriminatory relationships of whites with native Americans, blacks, and Chinese and Japanese immigrants. It took only a few acts of Congress to elevate racial feelings into laws against those immigrants who seemed different from white, Anglo-Saxon, Protestant Americans.

In 1882, in response to the clamor of white Californians, Congress prohibited further Chinese immigration. In 1907, a "gentleman's agreement" between the United States and Japan cut Japanese immigration to virtually zero.

Eastern European immigrants watched these developments with growing alarm. An 1891 article in a European Jewish journal, *Ha-Magid*, prophesied that discriminatory laws would soon be directed at Jews and other Europeans:

The United States of America is not what once it was: a land of fullest freedom, freedom of commerce, labor, residence, a land of one law for the native-born and the stranger. The laws against the Chinese and the pauper immigrants, tariffs on foreign products, the prohibition against imported labor—all show that even the Americans have learned to make a distinction between the native-born and the stranger. . . . A law to raise further the tariff on foreign goods is now being discussed . . . simply to close the doors to products of foreign manufacture. . . . When a nation begins to think in such terms, terms of we-they, it is not long before it proceeds from goods to people. . . . The day is near when the gates of the United States will be closed to immigrants, and not a vestige will remain of freedom of movement. The American legislature is already studying the question of immigration, examining the newcomers and their ways, to determine what kind of immigrant America should accept. As soon as they finish with the Chinese, they will turn to the Jews and the Italians and find all kinds of reasons for their exclusion.[7]

The regulation of European immigration began in 1875 with laws that declared prostitutes and convicts were ineligible to immigrate. In 1886, contract laborers were barred. These were immigrants who agreed to work for a year for low wages for agencies and companies who paid their fare from Europe. Employers had often imported contract laborers for use as strikebreakers, and the 1886 law seemed to benefit both exploited immigrants and struggling American workers alike. Other laws were aimed at keeping out "lunatics," "idiots," persons with symptoms of dangerous contagious diseases, and those who seemed likely to become "public charges." In time, anarchists and revolutionaries were added to the list of undesirables.

But how was an immigration official to determine which of the thousands of immigrants flooding Ellis Island each day were likely to become public charges? Decisions like this could be made arbitrarily, and one of the most important services that immigrant aid agencies performed was to try to insure that the decisions were made fairly.

In 1896, Congress set a standard for immigrant eligibility that was less open to interpretation: a literacy test. Senator Henry Cabot Lodge of Massachusetts led the fight for passage of the law and made clear just which immigrants the law was intended to bar:

The illiteracy [*sic*] test will bear most heavily upon the Italians, Russian, Poles, Hungarians, Greeks, and Asiatics, and very lightly, or not at all, upon English-speaking emigrants or Germans, Scandinavians, and French. In other words, the races most affected by the illiteracy test are those . . . who are most alien to the great body of the people of the United States. . . .

The statistics prepared by the committee show . . . that the immigrants excluded by the illiteracy test are those who . . . furnish . . . a large proportion of the population of the slums . . . those who bring the least money to the country and come most quickly upon public or private charity for support. . . .

. . . This bill, will operate against the most undesirable and harmful part of our present immigration and shut out elements which no thoughtful or patriotic man can wish to see multiplied among the people of the United States.[8]

President Grover Cleveland vetoed the literacy test:

It is said that the quality of recent immigration is undesirable. The time is quite within recent memory when the same thing was said of immigrants who, with their descendants, are now numbered among our best citizens.[9]

President William Howard Taft vetoed the next literacy test that Congress passed in 1913. Another was vetoed by President Woodrow Wilson in 1915.

Wilson's thinking had come some distance from the anti-immigrant sentiments he had expressed ten years earlier.

> This bill embodies a radical departure from the tradition and long established policy of this country. . . . It seeks to close all but entirely the gates of asylum which have always been open to those who could find [it] nowhere else . . . and it excludes those to whom the opportunities of elementary education have been denied without regard to their character, their purpose or their natural ability.[10]

But in 1917, just before the United States entered World War I, the restrictionist camp grew strong enough to override a second veto by President Wilson. The literacy test became law. Immigrants now would be required to read a forty-word passage in English or another language before they could gain admittance to the United States.

For four bloody years, the war in Europe put a halt to immigration. But after the war, immigrants once more trekked to the seaports to board ships to America. The literacy requirement proved easy to get around; people simply took the precaution of learning to read before they embarked.

The intense patriotism of wartime had heightened Americans' suspicion and dislike of foreigners. Anyone who was not "100 percent American" was more distrusted than ever. The Russian Revolution of

1917 added more fuel to the fire. Eastern European immigrants had always included a vocal minority of Socialists, anarchists, and revolutionary thinkers. Now that the Bolsheviks* had successfully staged a revolution in the Russian Empire, Americans feared that immigrant radicals would foment revolution here. This "Red Scare" led to a short period of roundups and deportations of immigrants suspected of radical beliefs. Over five thousand aliens, many of them Russian, were deported between December 1919 and March 1920. Living and working became more difficult than ever for Russians in the United States. A YMCA official who worked with Russian immigrants wrote:

> Since the "Bolshevik" regime began in Russia, the Russian is regarded everywhere as a "Bolshevik" and is shunned. I encountered a case the other day where an employer got the idea that the distinguishing feature of a "Bolshevik" was a beard, so he refused to give employment to some faithful and loyal Old Believers† whose religious conviction does not permit them to shave.[11]

* The Bolsheviks were members of the radical faction, led by V. I. Lenin, of the Russian Democratic Labor Party.

† Old Believers were dissenters from the Russian Orthodox Church and members of one of the several groups developed from the seventeenth-century schism in protest against liturgical reform. Many Old Believers preserved distinctive old-style dress and other traditions.

Rabid "Americanism" revived the Ku Klux Klan, an organization which had arisen in the South during Reconstruction to enforce white supremacy. The new Klan, reborn in 1915, added anti-Catholicism and anti-Semitism to its hate list, and during the 1920s counted some five million members in several southern and midwestern states. Ida Richter, a Russian-Jewish immigrant, experienced the Klan in action, when her husband moved the family from Chicago to the small town of Clinton, Illinois, to set up a business there.

[We were] there five years. . . . The Ku Klux Klan was very powerful in those days, 1923. And we used to have the KKK—three K's— on the sidewalk and the door. I went through anti-Semitism so much here because we lived in a Gentile neighborhood. There were only five Jewish families. . . .

Well, I seen how my children felt. One time, they read a story, "The Jew Among Thorns" in the textbook, and when [my daughter] went down to recess, they all pointed to her, she's a Jew, too. She said, "Mother, I felt so bad. Is it bad to be a Jew?" I told her, "It's nice to be a Jew. You're just as swell as anybody." She said, "But they look so funny at me." And when it was *Yom Kippur* and we observed that holiday . . . she laid on the couch and told her girlfriends she's sick; she didn't want to tell

them that we have a Jewish holiday. Now is
this a way to live for a Jew? That's why I
told [my husband], "We're going back to
Chicago."[12]

Most ominous for immigrants were a new set of
laws in the making. The first law, passed in 1921,
set the pattern that later laws would use. There
would be quotas for the number of immigrants of
each nationality that would be admitted to the
United States each year. In the 1921 formula, a
nation's quota was figured as 3 percent of the
foreign born of that nationality living in the United
States in 1910, as shown in the 1910 census. The
Johnson-Reed Immigration Act of 1924 reworked
the formula to limit a nation's quota to 2 percent of
the foreign born of that nationality as counted in
the 1890 census. This revision neatly reduced the
quotas for eastern Europeans by discounting the
nearly five million of them who had arrived from
1891 to 1910.

But the 1924 formula was only intended as a
temporary measure. The Johnson-Reed act also
created a commission to trace the nationalities of
the immigrant ancestors of all Americans listed in
the 1920 census. The final quotas would be based
on the percentage of the current American population that traced its ancestry back to each group. This
formula gave an overwhelming advantage to the
"Nordic" nationalities, for they had come earliest in

great numbers, and their descendants had multiplied over many generations.

The final quotas went into effect in 1929. Asian immigrants were excluded utterly. North and South Americans were exempt from the quota system in the interests of good inter-American relations. A ceiling of 150,000 was set for the number of Europeans who would be admitted each year. Of these 150,000 slots, 65,361—or 44 percent—were allocated to Great Britain. In contrast, Poland's quota was 6,524 (4 percent), and Russia's was 2,784 (barely 2 percent).

Katya Govsky, who left Russia in 1924, and had to sneak across borders as she made her way through Europe because she had left Russia illegally, said:

We came to Cherbourg, France, where we were to board our boat for the United States. The quota was closed, so we couldn't go. The White Star Line was responsible for us. They supported us all along because they sold us the tickets.

So they put us in quarantine in the Hotel Atlantique. We were at least two thousand immigrants, maybe more: Czechs, Rumanians, Greeks, Turks, what not. There were dormitories and fenced-in yards with guards. You couldn't go out and you couldn't come in. . . . Every morning, at seven o'clock, a loud bell rang and we all had to go through the showers and have a doctor's examination because you couldn't go to the United States if you had a disease. . . .

After about a year, we got out of the quarantine, and we rented an apartment . . . and lived there until 1929. . . . And then the papers came that we could go. . . . I was twenty-three years old.[13]

The quota system reversed the traditional immigration policy of the United States. Instead of beckoning welcome, the upraised arm of the Statue of Liberty now seemed to warn, "Stay back—unless you're British!" Even political and religious refugees were not exempt from the national quotas. This restriction would have particularly severe consequences for Europe's Jews during the Nazi era that loomed just beyond the 1929 quota system.

Eastern and southern European immigration dwindled to insignificance. England, Ireland, and Germany, which had the largest quotas, no longer suffered the same economic conditions that had sent millions of their citizens to the United States in the centuries past. In most years, these countries' quotas were only partially filled. The great tide of immigration had been stemmed. Oscar Handlin noted:

Probably the whole twenty-five year period after 1925 saw fewer newcomers to the United States than the single year 1907.[14]

Chapter 10

A New Dark Age in Europe

> Why? Why did we walk like meek sheep to the slaughter-house? Why did we not fight back? . . . Because we had faith in humanity. Because we did not really think that human beings were capable of committing such crimes.[1]
>
> GERDA KLEIN

Just as the gates to the United States closed down, eastern Europe was entering a period of great distress and upheaval, the cruelest in European history. Immigration declined steeply, not only because of restrictive U.S. immigration laws, but because new totalitarian governments in Europe were making it increasingly difficult to leave.

It started with World War I. The conflict sparked when a Serbian Nationalist assassinated the Austrian archduke in 1914. As England was pulled into the

176

war, Sir Edward Grey, the British foreign secretary,
reflected:

The lamps are going out all over Europe. We
shall not see them lit again in our lifetime.[2]

Four bloody years later, over ten million had
been killed, and more than twice as many scarred.
The lights went on again, but over a different
Europe.

For some eastern Europeans, the changes were at
first liberating. The czar of Russia was overthrown
by revolution in March 1917. Then early in 1919,
the peace settlements following World War I drastically altered the face of Europe by dismantling
countries, changing borders, and creating such
newly independent states as Poland, Czechoslovakia, Yugoslavia, Albania, Lithuania, Latvia, and
Estonia.

Eight months after the overthrow of the czar,
there had been a second revolution in Russia. The
Bolsheviks, led by V. I. Lenin, seized the government from more moderate parties, crushed their
enemies in a three-year civil war, and established
a Communist regime. In 1923, they declared the
formation of the Union of Soviet Socialist Republics.

For immigrant Katya Govsky, a Ukrainian Jew,
World War I, the Russian Revolution, and the civil
war that followed melted into one long siege of fear
and suffering. Govsky recalled the widespread
starvation during these years:

Oh my God! What I have seen with my own eyes. In the mud, dead horses were lying. With knives, people would take the meat and eat. Whatever they could find, they would eat—cats and dogs. . . . That's the most atrocious thing: to see people die from hunger. On one block, you'd see maybe five, ten people lying there.[3]

Many people resisted the Bolsheviks, and nowhere was the resistance more intense than in the Ukraine. In 1918, Ukrainian Nationalists had declared their desire for a "free Ukraine in a free Russia." They fought the Red Army for three years, but finally were forced to lay down their arms in 1921. Katya Govsky recalled:

The government was changing all the time. So one week we would go to school, and then two weeks, we couldn't, because there were fights in the streets. I was coming from school one day and all of a sudden, a grenade exploded and blew me against the wall. My whole side was full of metal splinters. My brother cut them out with a razor. I still have those scars.

. . . During the war, the Germans came and were raping women. The Bolsheviks were a relief because even if they confiscated everything from you, still and all, you were not afraid to walk on the streets and you were not afraid of being a Jew.* . . . The Bolsheviks were killing rich people. Because Pa was so good to his workers, they would not let the Bolsheviks kill him. They protected Pa.[4]

Many anti-Bolsheviks, and people who were simply nonpolitical but fearful, fled during these years of strife. Most of them settled in other parts of Europe. American immigration laws discouraged any large movement here.

Emigration from the new Soviet Union was not great for several reasons. Many people, happy to be rid of the czar, hoped that the new government would fulfill its promise: "Peace, Land, All Power to the Soviets†." Many people felt deep attachment to their homeland and did not wish to leave. Many didn't have the means to go: neither money nor relatives abroad to help them resettle. The United States was screening out immigrants from eastern Europe. The countries of western Europe were suffering their own postwar economic and political upheavals. There were not many places where refugees from the Soviet Union would be welcome. Finally, as the

---

* Govsky is referring to the pogroms staged by the Ukrainians. Their traditional anti-Semitism was intensified by their belief that the Jews were pro-Bolshevik. Some two hundred thousand Jews are estimated to have been killed in the Ukraine between 1918 and 1921.

† Local revolutionary councils of workers, peasants, or soldiers.

Communist government consolidated its rule, it became nearly impossible for Soviet citizens to leave, or even move about freely within the USSR.

The Communists had taken over an immense and poor country, devastated by war and revolution. They wanted to build a society in which no one was rich and no one was poor. At the outset, the government took over the property of the merchants, factory owners, and large landowners and ran the markets, factories, and farms. In an effort to put across Communist ideals, the government would go on to control the press, education, the arts, and the Church. It was a time of transition, and opposition came from many quarters. The Communists often dealt with the situation harshly, using force and terror.

Valery Arlan, a Russian Jew who was born around the time Katya Govsky emigrated, lived in the Soviet Union until 1974. He and his family experienced many of the terror campaigns of the Soviet government. He described how his family's troubles started:

It was the time of the Revolution. My father's family had a couple of cows. Therefore they were considered as rich. And because they were "rich," they were not treated well from the beginning. And my father understood then that it will be bad for them.

He passed then more years in this village. I was born there in 1928. That same year he left, in the middle of the night. The commissars and the police were coming after him. He left the village forever, and his three brothers left too. Because, right before this time, Lenin had permitted the NEP—New Economic Policy. Peasant families could maintain private farms and property. My father and his brothers were able to do well with this. But then the government turned against the NEP-men. When they gathered their crops, the government came and took everything. And they wanted to arrest them all.[5]

Josef Stalin, Lenin's successor in 1924, had re versed Lenin's economic policy. In 1928, he set out to transform the farms of the Soviet Union into collectives, believing this would lead to higher crop production. The peasants resisted—they wanted their own lands. Stalin dealt with them ruthlessly. Between 1929 and 1934, over ten million peasants were killed in Stalin's drive to collectivize agriculture. Many were executed outright; the rest died slowly in Siberian labor camps.

Stalin was a suspicious man, even paranoid, who never felt secure in his power. He believed he had enemies everywhere, threatening his rule. He dealt with them through wave after wave of party purges, arrests, imprisonments, and executions. One did not have to be an anti-Communist to be condemned as an enemy of the State. One needed only to be a member of a class or group that Stalin did not trust or like. There were wholesale roundups and arrests. He destroyed perhaps twenty million lives during his thirty years in power.

The late 1930s was a particularly fearful time. No segment of society was spared. Five thousand army officers were executed. Party officials were tortured to make them confess their crimes. Intellectuals, professionals, peasants, workers—all were terrorized by secret police raids. Ariana Arlan, Valery's wife, recalled:

In my childhood, about 1937, it was awful years. Every day, in every family, we were afraid that some day, some night, somebody will knock on the door and tell to my father, "Go with us." He was a doctor and head of a hospital. So if somebody will say something bad about him, that would be enough for him to be arrested. Many of our friends and relatives already had this trouble.

After those years, the head of the police—who was good with my father—showed him letters that had been written about him. He told my father, "I could have put you in prison with these letters." Anonymous letters. Nonsense about my father.

Those years are always with me. I couldn't talk about my grandfather who had been a rich man. No one should know about this! So from childhood you have this feeling—what you can speak and what you can't speak.[6]

World War I, the postwar economic depression, and repressive politics—all contributed to the extraordinary human toll in Russia during this period.

Western Europe too was struggling with disastrous economic conditions while new and ominous political events took shape in its midst. In 1933, Adolf Hitler and the Nazi party came to power in Germany. In less than ten years, they were the masters of most of Europe.

One by one, between 1938 and 1941, the countries of Europe fell to the Nazis. Over ten million eastern Europeans were to die in Nazi labor and death camps. More than twice as many died in the war it took to destroy the Nazi menace.

Shortly before Hitler invaded Poland in 1939 (he had already annexed Austria in 1936 and secured the Sudetenland from Czechoslovakia in 1938), he secretly agreed to divide Poland with the Soviet Union. Hitler hoped to keep Stalin from opposing him in Poland, since he did not want to wage war with the Soviet Union until sometime later. Germany and Russia signed a nonaggression pact to the astonishment of the world. The two countries were traditional enemies and, since the rise of Hitler, ideologically opposed to one another.

Rachel Simon, at that time a seventeen-year-old Polish citizen, told how these events first placed her under German and then under Russian authority:

In 1939, the first of September, the war broke out. After two weeks, the Germans came to our town. And every day there was something different written on those posters: The Jews have to come and register. The Jews have to bring their gold. The Jews have to give over their furs. The Jews have to clean up the streets and the factories. It was the beginning.

Four weeks after the Germans came into Poland, the Russians came in from the other side. Poland was divided in two parts. Our town was like a border town: still on the German side, but only a few miles from the Russian part of Poland.

One day, the Germans posted that all the Jews have to leave in 24 hours to go to the other side of Poland, the Russian part. I think they did this in all the border towns.

It started a terrible panic. Can you imagine —people that were living for ten generations in that town, they had to leave everything and go. You didn't know where you were going, and what's going to happen to our homes.

The older people—my mother and the neighbors—they decided that they would remain at home, and that the children should leave for the Russian side. . . . We thought that in a few days, the whole thing would quiet down, and we would come back home. Nobody imagined that here would be a Hitler, who would kill people for nothing! Who would kill young children, who would do such terrible things. In the beginning we did not understand what this Hitler was. We thought we would come back.

Rachel never saw her mother again. She and some of her brothers and sisters were put up by a Jewish family in a border town on the Russian side. Six months passed.

Then one day the Russian government started to register the refugees. And they asked us what we wanted to do. Did we want to stay with them in Russia? (They said this part of Poland was already Russia.) Did we want to be Russian citizens? Or did we want to go back to where we were born? We said we wanted to go home, to our families.

One night in May, the Russians took together all those people who wanted to go home, thousands of people, from all the towns around. They said to us, "You want to go home? You will go home!" They put us in big cattle cars. Sixty in one car—without toilets, without water, without anything. They pushed us in.

The train started to go. And we saw that we are not going home. We are going in a different direction.

They were going to Siberia. The journey took four months by train, boat, raft, cart, and foot.

What we went through till we came to Siberia, nobody can imagine. Once a day they opened the cars, and they threw in a few pieces of bread, like we were dogs, and some water. Once a day they opened the wagon so we should go out and go to the toilet. And there was, of course, no toilet. We ran out under the wagons and let down our pants. There was no shame anymore.

After three years in one camp, Rachel, one sister, and two brothers were released and sent to work in Yakutsk, an industrial city in eastern Siberia. There they spent the remainder of the war. It was only when the war was over that they learned how lucky they had been to be sent to Siberia.

We heard the war news in Yakutsk. But we didn't know what was happening to the Jews in Europe. Only later. My brother who sneaked back across the border from the Russian part of Poland—he died. And my mother. And my mother's sister who lived in the same town. She had eight children. Not one remained alive. All my neighbors. Nobody's alive. How many are alive from the whole Jews? We were lucky that we lived in that part of Poland that was near the border, and they threw us out, and they took us to Siberia. That's how we survived.[7]

Some six million Jews—70 percent of the Jewish population of Europe—did not survive. Millions of other Europeans, as well, were rounded up and killed by Nazis, or worked to death in their labor camps. Poles, Russians, Lithuanians, Gypsies, Communists, Socialists, Liberals, intellectuals, all the people of eastern Europe suffered great losses.

But it was different for the Jews. Hitler intended to exterminate them. In 1919, fourteen years before he became chancellor of Germany, Hitler wrote:

> [The] final objective must unswervingly be the removal of the Jews altogether.[8]

Hitler was obsessed with hatred for Jews. He preached to Germans his vision of a master race: the German people—ordained by God to rule over the inferior races of Europe. Jews were the enemies of this vision. While the German race represented perfection, the Jewish race represented evil. At the end of 1941, he gave orders for the "final solution" to the "Jewish question," code words for genocide.

At the height of the Nazi conquests, Hitler was master of Europe from France to western Russia, a territory encompassing over eight million Jews. Nazi control was most complete in eastern Europe. Since this area held the largest concentration of Jews in the world, most of the victims were eastern European Jews (see Appendix, Table 3: Estimated Jewish Population Killed in World War II).

As the German army swept across southern Russia in 1941, specially trained Nazi death squads accompanied the military. They had no combat assignment; their sole task was to kill Jews. Valery Arlan's father believed that Hitler meant what he said regarding Jews, and took his family far into the interior of Russia, beyond the German occupation,

practically into Asia. There they survived the war.
Years later, just before he emigrated, Arlan paid a
sentimental visit to the small Russian town where
he had been born, and which his parents fled when
he was just an infant. He learned what happened to
the Jews who remained there.

> We had come from a small village, a *shtetl,*
> near Smolensk. It had been very beautiful. But
> when I came back to that place, there was no
> village. All the houses were burned by the
> Germans. All the people were killed at a place
> about a mile and a half outside the village.
>   When I came to that place, I spoke with
> people who lived in the villages nearby. I said
> who I am. They said, "Oh, yes. We remember
> your grandfather." And then I asked, "Can
> you show me where was our house?" They
> showed me. There was only a stone. They said
> it was from the wall of the house. And then
> they told me what happened when the Germans
> came.
>   There was an order that all the Jews have
> to come to two houses. They came, and it was
> so crowded that they couldn't even sit. And
> they didn't allow them to leave these houses.
> There was no food, nothing. They suffered.
>   Then they gave an order for all the men who
> were there. The younger men had went to the
> war. These men were 40 and 50 years old.
> They told them that they have to work some-

where. They took them outside the village. They killed them in the forest.

Then only old, old people, and women and children were left. They told them that they are going to work, too. But just a little outside the village, they gave them an order to take off all their clothes. So they understood what was going to happen.

Pits were ready in that place. And that man who was telling me this story— he had dug these pits. And then two Russian policemen and two Germans came. They began to shoot the people.

They had mobilized the people from the villages around to bury the Jews. And the man who was telling me this was one of them. And he said, until this year, you could see the grave. But that this year, they planted potatoes on the place.

But I saw this place. And the leaves of the potatoes were a different color. They were a dark, dark green, and they were very strong leaves in this place.[9]

Auschwitz-Birkenau, Belzec, Chelmno, Majdanek, Sobibor, Treblinka were the killing centers the Nazis had erected in conquered Poland in 1942. Jews were transported there from all over the Nazi empire, gassed to death, and cremated. Only a small percentage of those taken to these places survived. The young and the strong were picked out to be used as a work force. Some of them managed to live through the horrors, along with some of the Jews and others who had been shipped to labor camps in Germany. Bitter memories haunt them.

Judith Newman recalled her arrival at Auschwitz:

> Corpses were strewn all over the road; bodies were hanging from the barbed-wire fence; the sound of shots rang in the air continuously. Blazing flames shot into the sky; a giant smoke cloud ascended above them. Starving, emaciated human skeletons stumbled toward us, uttering incoherent sounds. They fell down right in front of our eyes, and lay there gasping out their last breath.[10]

Gisella Perl, a prisoner-doctor at Auschwitz, described the deaths of a group of pregnant women:

> They were beaten with clubs and whips, torn by dogs, dragged around by the hair and kicked in the stomach. . . . Then, when they collapsed, they were thrown into the crematory —alive.[11]

A survivor of Dachau recalled:

> The SS* guards took pleasure in telling us that we had no chance of coming out alive, . . .

Schutzstaffel: formed as an elite guard, the SS also acted as security troops, guards in concentration camps, etc.

insisting that after the war the rest of the world would not believe what happened; there would be rumors, speculations, but no clear evidence, and people would conclude that evil on such a scale was just not possible.[12]

The world knew something of what was going on by the end of 1942. But it was not until Allied armies liberated the camps that people outside understood what this information really meant. Bergen-Belsen, in Germany, was the first concentration camp to be liberated. American historian Lucy Davidowicz, who worked at Belsen after the war in the relief effort for the survivors, described how the news was broken to the world:

On April 15, 1945, when the 11th Armored Division of the British Second Army entered Bergen-Belsen, they came upon 40,000 sick, starving, and dying prisoners . . . mostly Polish and Hungarian Jews, and 10,000 corpses stacked in high heaps. To be sure, in the hierarchy of horror, Belsen had ranked low. Auschwitz, Belzec, Chelmno, Majdanek, Sobibor, Treblinka—these were the great killing centers. . . . But the British had their first direct encounter with death camps at Belsen, and their shock made Belsen a byword for terror. The *Times* correspondent began his story: "It is my duty to describe something beyond the imagination of mankind."[13]

While British and American armies liberated western Europe, the Soviet Red Army freed eastern Europe from Hitler's grasp. In an abrupt turnabout on its ally, Germany had invaded the Soviet Union in June 1941 and kept up offensive action until the siege of Stalingrad (now Volgograd) ended in February 1943 with the surrender of a 300,000-man German army, exhausted by cold and starvation. From this point on, the Soviet army started to push the Germans back across eastern Europe. The Soviet and the American armies met near Berlin in April 1945. The end of the "Thousand Year Reich" (or Empire)* finally came with Germany's unconditional surrender in early May.

After the war, England, France, and the United States occupied western Germany and Austria and together with the Soviet Union administered Berlin. The Soviet Union had already occupied eastern Germany and much of eastern Europe and slowly began to form governments in all the eastern European countries. At first, governments incorporating many parties—Communists, Socialists, Liberals, Conservatives—were established in these lands. But later, Communists trained in Moscow took control of the major ministries: Defense (the army), In-

---

* At the 1934 Nazi Party Congress in Nuremberg, Hitler had proclaimed that with his coming to power the "German form of life is definitely determined for the next thousand years. . . . There will be no other revolution in Germany for the next one thousand years!"

terior (the police), and Justice (the courts). Gradually, with the backing of the Soviet troops that occupied their countries, the Communists stifled the press and crippled the opposition parties.

An immigrant to the United States, Stephen Lemkowski, a leader of the Polish Underground during the Nazi occupation, served in the postwar coalition government in Poland. He soon learned that his days there were numbered.

> I was arrested in 1945 as the head of the Polish Underground. Later on, the Communists decided to release me from prison, along with my wife, in order to create a better atmosphere, a kind of understanding and compromise. Then I entered politics, of course as an anti-Communist. I was a member of the Polish Peasant Party. . . . I delivered one speech in Parliament in which I criticized the Communist takeover. And so, I had to escape. I was warned by some people: "Your speech delivered in Parliament sealed your fate. Either you join the Communist Party or go abroad."[14]

Another immigrant, Bill Glass, a Hungarian Jew, survived a Nazi concentration camp, only to find himself subject to another form of persecution.

> I found that prior to the war I was hated because I was a Jew. And after the war I would be hated because I was a capitalist—or maybe

just a descendant of a capitalist. I was myself never a capitalist. We never had anything else but the bare existence, but my father was at one time in business. So we were capitalists as far as the communist system was concerned.

I saw that this system does not permit you to fulfill your personal capabilities. You had to be subject to their decisions, the communists. They would tell you where you are going to work and what you are going to work. . . .

I would always have been sort of a self-made man. I like to cut my own direction. And all of a sudden I find that I'm going to lose my identity. And I just don't want to live under the communist system. I fled in 1948.[15]

Communists were completely in control of the governments of eastern Europe by 1948. Romania, Hungary, Poland, Czechoslovakia, Yugoslavia, and East Germany became known as the "Iron Curtain" countries. Winston Churchill, who had been prime minister of England during the war, added that phrase to history:

A shadow has fallen upon the scenes so lately lighted by the Allied victory. . . . From Stettin in the Baltic to Trieste in the Adriatic, an iron curtain has descended across the Continent. Behind that line lie all the capitals of the ancient states of Central and Eastern Europe . . . in what I must call the Soviet sphere, and all are subject . . . not only to Soviet influence but to a very high, and . . . increasing measure of control from Moscow.[16]

A Hungarian immigrant, George Lavos, was a teen-ager when the Communists took over his country. He described how the change affected young people:

The Communists concentrated immediately on the youth. To change us in my age group—14 and 15—by then it was too late. We had belonged to a free society which was interrupted, and we resented this. So they started right away on the young ones, from the ages of six and seven. They created socialist youth camps by the hundreds. And socialist youth organizations which was teaching the children from Marx and Stalin, and brainwashing them against their own parents, if it had to be done. The education was completely changed. All the books were changed, except in math. I mean, history was changed. They might even change the outcome of historic battles if it suited their purpose. The Communist Party tried to teach us to believe in the dictatorship which they were trying to create. At the end of 1948, we saw that freedom of speech, freedom of communications and everything else, was cut out.

Lavos went on to explain how the party determined a young person's education and career:

In 1950, I graduated secondary school. By that time, the state was deciding who is going to the university and which one. They asked you to which one you would like to go, but that was completely meaningless. If you wanted to be an engineer, and they thought to make a doctor out of you—you were told that you just had to become a doctor. And you would make a face. Then they would say, "Well, then you have another choice, my friend. You can go down into the factory." And so there was no choice.

And then there was one more thing which they screened: the class background. If your father was an officer in the old Hungarian Army, or a landowner, or he had a little shop, he was called a capitalist, a non-reliable element; and he wasn't trusted. Myself, I wasn't trusted.

Shortly after he started the university, Lavos was drafted into the army. There he got into trouble.

I went into the Hungarian army for 3½ years. When I came out they threw me into political prison for a year for some statements which I made in my last year in the army. I was a sergeant, and I didn't like things. And the division party secretary and me weren't on very friendly terms. I always had a loud mouth, and I opened it. So they discharged me, and put me to trial as a "fascist element." I got one year.

I was lucky to get one year on a political charge.[17]

In 1952, Stalin was preparing another great purge in the Soviet Union. First he struck at Communist party officials whom he suspected of disloyalty. Next he accused a group of Kremlin doctors, most of whom were Jews, of trying to poison the country's leaders. Two of the doctors died under torture; the rest confessed to the trumped-up charge. Stalin was beginning to reach beyond the Kremlin (the fortress-like building that is the center of the government in Moscow), when he died in March 1953. It was during this last purge that Valery Arlan had an encounter with the secret police.

It was the last year of Stalin's life. He began to destroy the Jewish community—the best, the most talented Jews. He killed them, just killed them. In the morning, about six o'clock, the radio would begin. And you would hear: "The killers in white robes—the Jewish doctors!" It was a lie, you knew. But a lot of people believed it.

I was working at a plant near Moscow, as an industrial engineer. A lot of us were sent there from the university, and we lived around the plant. One day, a girl came to me and said, "You have to go to headquarters."

I asked, "Why?"

She said, "You will go and you will know why."

I went into a room, and a man was sitting there in uniform. He came from Moscow. The first question was, "Why did you come to this plant?"

"Why? They sent me! You don't know this?"

And then he said, "We have some special data that you want to make an explosion in the plant on the day of Stalin's death."

"Me?"

And he began to tell me how I wanted to do it. That I didn't tell the workers that they have to have special safety devices. That I didn't tell them on purpose. And that this could lead to an explosion.

It was not my responsibility at all to look at this equipment.

I left the plant and I went home, and I was lying in my room and I was very pale. And then the door opened and it was a friend who finished the university with me. Another Jew. And I saw that he was pale, too.

He told me that they called him. He was the head of a shop that used chemicals. And they told him that he used these chemicals as a poison in the dining room, in order to kill the workers.

Arlan and his friend sweated out the next few weeks, waiting to be called again before the secret police.

But just as Kremlin politics had first placed them in danger, a change in Kremlin politics saved them.

> After a few weeks [Lavrenti] Beria, the head of the KGB*, was arrested, and very soon killed. It was just a competition between the factions in the government. And the government wanted to show it was the end of Beria's policy. So we were free. All the charges against us disappeared. Those people who interrogated us, they were killed with Beria.[18]

George Popescu, a Romanian who immigrated to the United States in 1976, believes fear of Soviet intervention keeps present government in power.

> I'd say over 90 percent of the people are against the Communist government. One of the things under the Communist system, there is a fear. You never know who will come if the head of the government falls. You never know if the Russians will come from outside and take the country under their kind of tutelage. And this is something that the government and the Communist Party are using against the people. "Okay," they say. "This is bad. But it could be worse." So this is how they keep the people quiet.[19]

Fear is what twentieth-century eastern European immigrants talk about. Fear of the army, the police,

* State security police.

the government. Ariana Arlan, Valery's wife, told how her fear remained with her for a long time after she came to the United States:

> It seems to me only now, after five years, that I feel myself free from these constant feelings of being afraid of something. Afraid to speak to people, afraid something could happen from every side. I felt it all the time in Russia.[20]

Stanislaw Walesa, who came to Jersey City, New Jersey, from Poland in 1973, has had a difficult experience. With the rest of the world he watched and waited in August 1980 while his son, Lech Walesa, led hundreds of thousands of Polish workers in Gdansk on a successful strike against the government for—among other demands—the right to have independent unions in Poland. While the final outcome of the strike may not be known for some time, this proud father stated at the time:

> I am elated it all worked itself out in the best interest of Polish workers. The future is bright now and largely because of my son. I love my country. I want to return to my roots.[21]

Mr. Walesa died in Jersey City in 1981.

Chapter 11

Survivors and Dissidents

A small group of men dressed in new Bulgarian-made suits walked quietly out of a . . . hotel very early yesterday and began a brief walk in the bright sunshine. Only hours earlier, they had stepped off a Soviet airliner and achieved a rare and precious status— former political prisoner. . . .

Later, at a news conference . . . [Jewish activist Eduard S. Kuznetsov] said he understood that the United States, being no "paradise on earth," had problems. "These are liberty's burdens, which are not easy but which cannot be compared with the heavy weight of un-freedom," he said.[1]

The New York Times

Immigration fell off drastically after 1929. The national origins quotas made it difficult for eastern

201

Europeans to enter the United States. Then the Nazi conquests, World War II, and the policies of the postwar Communist governments made it difficult for eastern Europeans to leave.

There would never again be anything like the great waves of immigrants that came between 1870 and 1924. Eight million eastern Europeans arrived during these five and a half decades. Only about a half million were able to come in the five decades afterward.

Perhaps the cruelest aspect of the national origins quota system was that there were no exceptions made for political and religious refugees. After Hitler became chancellor of Germany in 1933, Jews clamored to get out of the country. As he made aggressive moves toward eastern Europe, Jews there sought to escape. But few countries took in any great numbers of them. For its part, the United States refused to bend the quotas for these doomed people. Although concerned American Christians joined with American Jews to urge that the quotas be loosened during this time of crisis, the restrictionists remained firm. Congressman Martin Dies of Texas stated:

We must ignore the tears of sobbing sentimentalists and internationalists, and we must permanently close, lock and bar the gates of our country to new immigration waves and then throw the keys away.[2]

Yet room could have been made for refugees from central and eastern Europe, not only Jews, but others whose lives were threatened by Nazism as well. The annual limit of 150,000 immigrants allowed by the 1929 law was never reached in any year before World War II. In some years, more immigrants left the country than arrived. Great Britain and Ireland, which had the largest quotas, used only half of the places allotted to them. But restrictionists would not allow the unused slots to be reassigned to other Europeans. The prejudice against eastern Europeans and Jews played a definite part in this policy.

It was even hard for Europeans to be admitted within their national quotas. From 1929 to 1939, the United States was in the throes of the Great Depression, which kept millions of Americans unemployed. As a result, the government stiffened the income requirements for immigrants, so that they would not add to the public relief rolls. Red tape procedures caused difficulties as well. After 1929, would-be immigrants had to obtain visas, or immigration permits, from American consulates abroad. They had to give the consulates police certificates to testify to their character. It was often impossible for people who were being persecuted by their own governments to obtain the necessary documents. Such policies might not be subject to criticism under normal circumstances. But Europe in the 1930s was not normal.

Valery Gogalack was one of the eastern Europeans who was able to go to the United States in the 1930s. Unlike so many Europeans at this time, he was not a political or religious refugee.

I was an engineer in Poland. I built big cranes in the port of Gdynia. Then I started building the bridge on the river Dniester. And when I finished that, I went to make a design of a reinforced concrete skyscraper in Warsaw. And when I finished all these works, I had an invitation to study in America.

I came first of all to visit, as a student. I came on a boat from Danzig, on which you find those emigrants who knew that they wanted to go away for good and who finally got the visa to go to America. All of them were thinking that they go to a paradise. Everyone who was in America, he wrote to Poland that he gets here very good wages. And when you transfer the dollars to *zlotys* it was a fortune. So therefore, the immigrant thought that when he comes here, he is probably going to be a millionaire very soon. I didn't think this, because I knew exactly the things which happened here. I knew that I have to work very hard in order to be like any other engineer here.

The longer I was here, the more I liked America. And even I was twice, before the war, in Poland, and each time, when I was going back to America, I was very, very happy about it. Here I can really make something of myself. I can go higher. Being an engineer, I have tremendously big possibilities. I don't have any in Poland at this time. Say, roads— you practically didn't have roads in Poland. Or dams—one dam for the whole Poland. So there you are! If you build one dam, then that's the end of it.

Gogalack helped other Poles to emigrate as well.

America gave me new opportunity, and not only to me, but to thousands of Poles who during the war had to migrate here—the Polish intelligentsia, which couldn't find a place any more in Poland. When I knew that there were so many engineers stranded in France as exiles from Poland at the end of the war, I wanted them to come here. I organized a Polish engineering society in New York called *Polonia Technia,* and through this society I brought here 47 engineers. And I also went to the engineering societies here and asked them for support to find some work for those Polish engineers who came here.[3]

When the war ended, Europe was awash with refugees: eastern Europeans who survived Germany's forced labor camps; Jews who had lived through the Holocaust; political exiles who had escaped Nazi occupation and who did not wish to return to their countries to live under communist governments; eastern Europeans who fled west as the Iron Curtain rang down.

One million refugees had no place to go. They were housed in Displaced Persons (DP) camps in western Europe and clothed and fed by refugee relief organizations. The plight of these homeless, desperate people caused the first openings in U.S. immigration policy.

President Harry S Truman issued an emergency directive at the end of 1945 to admit 40,000 refugees. To do more, he needed an act of Congress, and restrictionist sentiment was still strong there. Truman finally got a Displaced Persons Act passed in 1948. It was not as far-reaching as he had wanted, but it was better than nothing. It allowed the admission of 410,000 DPs over a four-year period. When the DP Act expired in 1953, Congress enacted the Refugee Relief Act, which admitted an additional 189,000.

When Rachel Simon traveled some five thousand miles from Yakutsk in Siberia, to a DP camp near Frankfurt, Germany, she would discover that this was the beginning of her journey to America.

At the end of the war, Poland made an agreement with Russia to send back all the Polish people to Poland, in exchange for the Russians who were still in Poland. The Russians asked us to become Russian citizens. We didn't want

it. A lot of people went to jail for it. It was a
hard thing getting out of Russia and back to
Poland.

But when we came to Poland, a new agony
started. The Polish people didn't like the Jews
coming back. They were scared that they
would have to give back everything that they
robbed from us. The Polish people started
killing us, the refugees, on all the roads. So
we started to run again from Poland.

In Germany there were DP camps for
refugees who wanted to emigrate someplace.
And from there, people went to Israel and
America. It wasn't easy getting through Poland
to Germany. Israelis organized us—the
Haganah*—and took us across the border to
Czechoslovakia at night, and then into
Germany. We had to go into Germany
illegally, too, because there was no way to go
legally.

We finally got to the DP camp. We were
there for a year. I got married there. I had met
my husband in Siberia.

We wanted to go to Israel. But my sister,

* The militia of the Jewish community in Palestine.
Great Britain administered Palestine until May 1948. In
spite of the Palestinians' protests, Britain allowed 600,000
Jews to go there. The Jewish community sent Haganah
units to Europe to help refugees to get to the DP camps,
and then to smuggle them from there into Palestine.

who was already there, wrote that all the people who come go right to the war*, and that we should wait. We should go first to America because my husband could get in there. He was born in Germany, and with a German passport, you can go very easy into America at this time. So we didn't think of staying here. We were dreaming of going to Israel all our lives. But we stayed.[4]

Bill Glass, who fled Hungary in 1948, described his escape:

I was in business at the time. From 1946 till 1948, we were able to bring into the country various goods which Hungary did not have. The government permitted it on the basis that we had to pay duties of half the commodities brought in. Even this way, we were able to make a profit and we lived quite well. So because I was dealing with import merchandise, I spent a lot of time on the various borders. I made friends with a border guard, with a purpose. I knew what I was going to use him for. We wined together and established a friendship.

I chose the festive night of Christmas, when everybody was so jolly. After a couple of

* The war with the Palestinians and their Arab neighbors that followed the creation of Israel by the United Nations.

drinks, I said I would like to see how the other side lives in Slovakia. He said, "Why don't you go over and take a look?" So I went over, and I never returned.

I had a forged Hungarian passport. It was forged in Paris, where a friend of mine sent it down to me. It legalized my stay in Czechoslovakia, and then, when I went to Vienna, in Austria.

In 1949, Vienna was still occupied by the four Allied powers—Britain, France, the United States, and the USSR. Many eastern European refugees from communism came there, hoping to cross to one of the western-controlled sectors of the city. Officially classified as a refugee, Bill Glass was helped by the IRO (International Relief Organization) and eventually went to the United States.

Later, Bill Glass became involved in the next great European refugee crisis—the flight of some two hundred thousand Hungarians after their 1956 revolution was crushed by Soviet tanks and troops.

I became a [U.S.] citizen in 1956—July. And I wasn't planning any trips. Yet I applied for a passport. I just cannot explain that feeling that a Hungarian has about a passport, from that background. Having that passport enabled me in about two hours' notice to be on a plane and go back to Europe. And I brought my family out.

I left three sisters in Hungary. They were

married, and all of them had families. Then, in October, 1956, I got word that there is a revolution in Hungary, and I probably could bring my family out. The same night I took a plane. Twelve hours later I was at the bridge in Andau [Austria] where the people were fleeing from Hungary. I sent messages to my family that I am there and they should come. And they did come, and I helped them to come over to the States.[5]

The Hungarian revolution of 1956 had had its beginnings a year earlier, when the popular premier, Imre Nagy, was removed from office and replaced by a harder-line Communist more acceptable to Moscow. Students, workers, and writers began to hold meetings and draft resolutions in protest. George Lavos was there at a mass meeting in Budapest in October 1956.

When the 23rd of October came a peaceful meeting was allowed at General Bem's* monument at the outskirts of our great university in Budapest. They were expecting maybe four or five hundred youths to come and place a few flowers, because it was the anniversary of his birthday. Instead, all of a sudden, thousands and thousands of people came. They were called the night before to

* A Polish general who helped Hungarians in the revolution of 1848.

come and participate in this first free assembly since 1948. . . .

I was in one of the largest factories—a shipyard with 10,000 workers. And when we heard about the demonstration, at least half of us said we'd go when we finished up. At four o'clock, the suburbs, the outskirts of the city, and the industrial sections began to move. By the time this group reached Budapest, we were about 200,000 people. And instead of going to the monument, we went to the square outside the Hungarian Parliament. It was jammed with about 200 to 250 thousand people by six o'clock. That's when this big mass started to demand, "Let's hear Imre Nagy!" And the secret police brought Imre Nagy immediately from his house, because they got scared. They brought him just to calm the people.

But the demonstrators wanted more than Nagy. They wanted changes in the government

By the time they brought Imre Nagy to the steps of the Parliament, the first paper with the ten demands was already drawn: Out with the Russian troops! Freedom of press! Freedom of assembly! Freedom of religion! And so on. And these demands were read to the people.

And then it started. First the shouting, "Russians go home!" And then they cut out the communist symbol from the middle of the flags. . . . And the next step, that was the real dramatic step: We are going to send a delegation to the radio. Let the radio broadcast this meeting's resolutions, and then we can dissolve.

A delegation of five thousand people marched to the radio station. The first shots were fired there.

The secret police got scared, and they started to shoot. The news spread back that they are massacring members of the delegation, they are shooting them down. Which was true and wasn't true, because only two or three people got hit. But now the whole mass—two or three hundred thousand people marched to the radio station.[6]

Hungarian troops were sent to control the crowd, but they joined the demonstrators instead. By three o'clock in the morning, the crowd had taken the radio station. Later that day, Soviet troops that had been stationed in Hungary were dispatched to stop the demonstrations. But they were reluctant to fire on the people among whom they had been living. Some even joined the Hungarians. The government of Hungary was in a state of collapse.

Revolutionary councils formed, first in Budapest, then in several other parts of the country. They functioned as local governments, keeping order and distributing food. Imre Nagy formed a new national government which announced democratic reforms and began to negotiate with Moscow for the withdrawal of Soviet troops. George Lavos remembers this as, "the most beautiful life Hungary ever experienced from the second World War on, because it was complete freedom." But while Nagy was negotiating the withdrawal of Soviet troops in Hungary, fresh troops from the Soviet Union were being quietly moved to Hungary's borders. On the night of October 31 they crashed across. By November 4, they controlled most of the country.

Only a few pockets of resistance remained. One of these was the New Pest section of Budapest, where George Lavos was a member of the revolutionary council. Voice of America broadcasts, beamed from western Europe, urged the Hungarian rebels to keep fighting, and promised western assistance. But when Imre Nagy appealed to the United Nations for help against the Soviet forces, no help came. George Lavos described the final days of the revolt:

A lot of unnecessary bloodshed could have been avoided if between the 4th and the 15th of November the Voice of America wouldn't have broadcast those announcements that there are American units coming and volunteers by the hundreds of thousands, and to just go and keep up fighting. This was done by some very irresponsible people.

In New Pest, we had barricaded ourselves,

and we were waiting, because we were listening
to these broadcasts. On the 13th of November,
we had one of our last council meetings, and
we decided to form a delegation to try to crash
through to Vienna and find out what's the real
position. I was elected with two of my
comrades.

It took us about 28 hours—by foot, train,
bicycles, motor bicycles, anything—to reach
the border and come across. In Vienna, I saw
with my own eyes that there is no hope. Then
I made a broadcast on the Voice of America:
"Don't wait for the drums. Just put them
away." This was the signal, and the next day,
New Pest surrendered.[7]

By the end of November, Imre Nagy had been
arrested by the Soviets. He was later put to trial and
executed. George Lavos, safe and free in Vienna,
decided to go to the United States. Thirty thousand
Hungarian refugees were admitted to the United
States immediately after the revolution by order of
President Eisenhower, through a loophole in the
immigration law. More were admitted over the next
few years through special legislation passed by
Congress.

The Hungarian revolution refugees were the
closest thing to a "wave" of immigrants from eastern
Europe in the postwar era. Through the 1960s, the
number of immigrants from most of the Communist
countries were counted in the hundreds, not in

larger figures. Only Poland and Yugoslavia allowed more sizable emigration. Poland, because so many Poles had relatives here; and Yugoslavia because it had set out on its own kind of communism. Marshal Tito, Yugoslavia's leader, repudiated Soviet control and allowed the people greater freedom of movement than any other Communist country. Even so, the numbers from these countries were usually no more than five thousand a year.

When the state of Israel was founded in 1948, many Russian Jews began to feel that it was their real homeland. Over the years, they agitated for the right to emigrate to Israel. Then the United States and other governments applied political and economic pressure to move the Soviet authorities to allow Jews to leave. Finally, in the early 1970s, the Russian Jews began to come out. Most have gone to Israel, but about 15 percent of the two hundred thousand Jews who left in the 1970s eventually came to the United States.

On the whole, the DPs and dissidents of the postwar period made out better economically in the United States than the earlier generations of immigrants had. The majority of the prequota arrivals had been peasants. The later comers tended to be city people, from the middle and upper classes. They were better educated and often had professions. They could make good livings more easily than the earlier immigrants in the United States, not only because they were better prepared, but because there were fewer of them competing for American jobs and American sympathy. Polish immigrant Valery Gogalack continued his engineering career in the U.S. Hungarians Bill Glass and George Lavos each managed in time to start his own business.

Rachel Simon found it harder than these others. Even so, her living and working conditions were far superior to those the early immigrants had found.

It was a hard, hard life when we came. We didn't have any professions. We had both been students before the war. I was pregnant when I came [to New York] in 1948. But I had no money. So I went to work, and every day I was vomiting on the bus. We lived in a fourth-floor walk-up apartment, without heat or warm water, with two rooms and a bathtub in the kitchen. I had my first child there. It was really hard times.

My husband was sent to training school by the Hebrew Immigrant Aid Society. He learned how to push through a seam on a sewing machine. And that's how he has been sitting for 25 years—pushing that same seam. We never made big things, but we somehow managed to bring up two daughters.

When the children were small, I went to work at night, and then later I worked in the day when they were at school. I worked in a bakery. They taught me how to sell a roll in English and how to sell bread. "Bread" and "roll" were my first English words.

Every day I got more used to everything
here. And I love America, I really do. I was
never hungry here. I was never without clothes.
Somehow we managed to have what we need
and to give the children what they need.[8]

On October 3, 1965, President Lyndon B.
Johnson signed a new immigration law in a cere-
mony at the base of the Statue of Liberty. Presidents
Truman, Eisenhower, and Kennedy before him had
urged that the national origins be scrapped. President
Johnson finally helped it happen.

The new law still placed numerical limits on
immigration. No more than 20,000 a year could be
admitted from any country of Europe, Asia, and
Africa, and no more than 120,000 a year total
would be admitted from the countries of the
Western Hemisphere. But the law no longer played
favorites with nationalities. It no longer implied, as
President Truman had put it,

that Americans with English or Irish names
were better people and better citizens than
Americans with Italian or Greek or Polish
names.[9]

For many reasons, the great waves of immigration from eastern Europe are long past. One can
still find foreign-speaking communities of eastern
European immigrants, but they are small and few.
Some immigrants still gravitate to close, tight communities, where they can maintain the old ways.

But many of the later immigrants stayed aloof from the older immigrant communities. Class differences were often a factor in this. Another was that over time, the ethnic communities had lost a lot of their Old World character. Then, too, the newer immigrants were usually better equipped to manage here, and didn't require the same community support that earlier generations had.

There is no way to talk about the growth and development of the United States without coming again and again to immigrants' contributions. There is no way to talk about the American people without acknowledging that they mingle many ethnic traditions and points of view. The tolerance of diversity is what attracted so many people from so many lands to this country. And the presence of this diversity in our society is what keeps the tolerance strong. *E pluribus unum*—"one out of many"—is the Latin motto engraved on the seal of the United States. The American way of life has been nourished from many sources, and eastern Europe is notable among them.

APPENDIX

TABLE 1
Present-day Nations of Eastern European Populations

Country Today	*Political History*	*Resident Populations* (pre World War II)
Belorussian Soviet Socialist Republic (USSR)	Conquered in fourteenth century by Lithuania, which merged with Poland in 1569. With partitions of Poland in late eighteenth century (see Poland) passed to Russian Empire. Declared independence in 1918 after Russian Revolution, but retaken by Red Army. Belorussian SSR joined USSR in 1922.	Belorussians Jews (significant minority)
Bulgaria	Absorbed into Ottoman Empire end of fourteenth century. Semi-independent northern Bulgarian state, still tied to Turkey, set up after Turkish defeat in Russo-Turkish War, 1878. Annexed remaining Turkish territory 1885. Declared independence 1908. Macedonian region, liberated from Turks in 1913, disputed and divided among Greece, Bulgaria, and Yugoslavia.	Bulgarians Macedonians

Czechoslovakia	Created in 1918 from provinces of Austro-Hungarian Empire, after empire's defeat in World War I. SLOVAKIA had been ruled by Hungary since tenth century. CZECH provinces of BOHEMIA, MORAVIA, and CZECH SILESIA had been subject to Austria since sixteenth century.	Czechs Slovaks Jews (significant minority)
Estonia (USSR)	Taken by Russia from Sweden in 1710. Declared independence in 1918 with breakdown of Russian Empire after World War I defeat and Russian Revolution. Returned to Russian control by Nazi-Soviet Pact of 1939, and in 1940 incorporated into the Soviet Union.	Estonians
Hungary	Subject to Austria, after liberated by Austria from Turkish rule in 1699. Hungarian agitation for independence accommodated by "Compromise of 1867," when Hungary made junior partner in newly created Austro-Hungarian Monarchy. Became independent republic in 1919, after dissolution of	Magyars (historical, traditional name of Hungarians) Jews (significant minority)

Country Today	Political History	Resident Populations (pre World War II)
	Austro-Hungarian Empire at end of World War I.	
Latvia (USSR)	Portion of Latvia taken by Russia from Sweden in 1721. Remainder belonged to Poland, but with partition of Poland in eighteenth century (see Poland) fell to Russia. Declared independence in 1918 on breakdown of Russian Empire after World War I defeat and Russian Revolution. Reoccupied by Soviet Union in 1940 and incorporated into USSR.	Latvians Jews (significant minority)
Lithuanian Soviet Socialist Republic (USSR)	After two centuries of close alliance, merged with Poland in 1569. Thereafter, Poland dominated Lithuania. When Poland partitioned by European powers 1772–1795 (see Poland) Lithuania taken by Russia. Became independent republic on breakdown of Russian Empire 1918. Reoccupied by USSR in 1940 (World War II) and after war became constituent republic of USSR.	Lithuanians Jews (significant minority)

Poland

Powerful empire of fifteenth century gradually dismantled by expansion of neighbors. Austria, Russia, and Prussia divided Poland among themselves in three successive partitions—1772, 1793, and 1795. Poland ceased to exist. The largest part was absorbed into Russian Empire; the province of Galicia went to Austria; and two western provinces went to Prussia. (Prussia later became the nucleus of the German Empire in 1871.) The state of Poland was reestablished after the defeats of the Russian, Austrian, and German empires in World War I.

Poles
Jews (significant minority)

Romania

Of Romania's three major provinces, TRANSYLVANIA was occupied by the Magyars in the Middle Ages and held by Hungary until 1918; and MOLDAVIA and WALLACHIA were conquered by the Turks in the fifteenth and sixteenth centuries. After the Russo-Turkish War of 1828–1829, Moldavia and Wallachia gained a large degree of self-rule, though

Romanians
Magyars
(significant minority)
Jews (significant minority)

Country Today	*Political History*	*Resident Populations* (pre World War II)
	technically still part of the Turkish Empire, and very much dominated by Russia. The provinces were united as Romania in 1861, and after Turkey's defeat in the Russo-Turkish War of 1878, gained full independence. Romania annexed Transylvania from Hungary after Hungary's defeat in World War I, and obtained portions of other former Austro-Hungarian provinces with Romanian populations.	
Russian Soviet Federated Socialist Republic (USSR)	In the nineteenth century, the Russian Empire encompassed northern Europe east of the Baltic Sea and extended through Siberia to the Pacific Ocean. The czar was the absolute ruler. Minority populations were persecuted by the state, which hoped to "Russianize" its subject peoples. Czar Nicholas II was overthrown by the Russian Revolution of	Russians Significant minorities: Jews, Lithuanians, Poles, Ukrainians

February 1917. The democratic-leaning government which took power was itself overthrown by the Bolshevik (or Communist) Revolution of October 1917. The Bolsheviks declared the Russian Soviet Socialist Republic. In 1922, three other Soviet Socialist Republics—Armenian, Belorussian, and Ukrainian (all lands formerly subject to the czar)—joined the Russian SFSR to form the Union of Soviet Socialist Republics. The USSR, with the Russian SFSR at the head, now consists of fifteen Soviet Socialist Republics.

Ukrainians
Ruthenians (western Ukrainians)
Jews (significant minority)

Ukranian Soviet Socialist Republic (USSR)

Ukrainians and Russians formed one nation until the Mongol conquest of the early Russian state in the thirteenth century. Ruthenia, or western Ukraine, then conquered by Magyars and stayed under Hungarian rule until 1918. The major part of the Ukraine fell to Polish rule. Russia took a portion of this area after a war with Poland in 1667. With the par-

Country Today	Political History	Resident Populations (pre World War II)
	titioning of Poland in the late eighteenth century, most of the Ukraine went to Russia, but the region of east Galicia fell to Austria. In 1919, with the breakdown of the Russian and Austro-independent republic, Ukrainians declared an independent republic. But the Red Army won the conflict that followed, and in 1922, the Ukraine became part of the USSR.	
Yugoslavia	A federation of six republics created from Balkan states and provinces at the end of World War I. SERBIA, the largest of the Yugoslav republics, won independence from the Ottoman Empire in 1879. The only other Yugoslav state that was free at the start of World War I was MONTENEGRO, which had successfully resisted Ottoman conquest. CROATIA was ruled by Hungary. Present-day Croatia includes the former	Serbs Croats Dalmatians Slavonians Montenegrins Slovenes Macedonians Jews (significant minority)

provinces of **DALMATIA** (Austrian rule) and **SLAVONIA** (Hungarian rule). **SLOVENIA** belonged to the Austrian Empire. **MACEDONIA** was under Turkish rule. Greece, Bulgaria, and Yugoslavia all laid claim to Macedonia, and after World War I, it was divided among these three nations. **BOSNIA-HERZEGOVINA** (which despite its name was and is one province) had a mixed Serbian and Croatian population. It was freed from Turkish rule in 1878, but only to fall to Austrian occupation. It remained in the Austrian Empire until the end of World War I.

TABLE 2
Religions in Eastern Europe in the Nineteenth Century

Empires	*Orthodox*	*Subject Provinces* *Catholic*	*Protestant*	*Muslim*
Ottoman Empire (Muslim)	Bulgaria			Bosnia-Herzegovina* (about 40 percent of population converted to Islam after Ottoman conquest)
	Wallachia and Moldavia			
	Serbia			
	Macedonia			
	Bosnia-Herzegovina* (About 60 percent of population)			
Russian Empire (Orthodox)	Belorussia	Poland	Estonia	
	Ukraine	Lithuania	Latvia	

			Hungary (about one-third of population)
Austrian Empire (Catholic)	Poland	Hungary (about two-thirds of population)	
		Bohemia, Moravia, and Czech Silesia	
		Dalmatia	
		Slovenia	
Hungarian Empire (Catholic and Protestant)	Transylvania	Slovakia	
		Croatia	
		Slavonia (mixed Catholic and Orthodox population)	
Prussian Empire (Germany) (Protestant)	Poland		

* Taken from Ottoman Empire by Austria in 1878.

TABLE 3*
Estimated Jewish Population
Killed in World War II

Country	Estimated 1939 Jewish Population	Estimated Jewish Population Killed
Poland	3,300,000	3,000,000
Soviet Union	2,850,000	1,252,000
Hungary	650,000	450,000
Romania	600,000	300,000
Baltic countries	253,000	228,000
Czechoslovakia	180,000	155,000
Yugoslavia	43,000	26,000
Bulgaria	64,000	14,000

* Adapted from Lucy S. Davidowicz, *The War Against the Jews 1933–1945* (New York: Holt, Rinehart & Winston, 1975), p. 403.

Notes

Introduction: A New Immigration
1. Jean de Crèvecoeur, *Letters from an American Farmer* (London: 1782); reprinted in George McMichael, ed., *Anthology of American Literature,* Vol. 1 (New York: Macmillan Publishing Co., 1974), p. 432. (Spelling and punctuation have been modernized.)
2. Woodrow Wilson, *A History of the American People,* Vol. 5 (New York: Harper & Bros., 1902), pp. 212–213.

Chapter 1. The Political Landscape of Eastern Europe
1. Joseph A. Wytrwal, *America's Polish Heritage: A Social History of the Poles in America* (Detroit: Endurance Press, 1961), p. 293.
2. Ibid., pp. 127–128.
3. Ibid., p. 138.
4. Louis Adamic, *Laughing in the Jungle: The Autobiography of an Immigrant in America* (1932;

reprint ed., New York: Arno Press, 1969), pp. 25–28.

5. Bernard Pares, *A History of Russia* (New York: Vintage Books, 1965), p. 352.

Chapter 2. Roots: Peasant Life in Eastern Europe

1. Emily Greene Balch, *Our Slavic Fellow Citizens* (New York: Arno Press and The New York Times, 1969), p. 39.

2. Quoted in Doreen Warriner, *Contrasts in Emerging Societies* (Bloomington: Indiana University Press, 1965), p. 54.

3. Jerome Davis, *The Russian Immigrant* (New York: Arno Press and The New York Times, 1969), pp. 205–206.

4. Thomas Capek, *The Cechs (Bohemians) in America* (Boston: Houghton Mifflin Co., 1920), pp. 53–54.

5. William L. Thomas and Florian Znaniecki, *The Polish Peasant in Europe and America,* Vol. 1 (New York: Octagon Books, 1974), p. 345.

6. Davis, *The Russian Immigrant,* p. 202.

7. Kenneth D. Miller, *Peasant Pioneers: An Interpretation of the Slavic Peoples in the United States* (San Francisco: R & E Associates, 1969), pp. 16–17.

8. Ibid., p. 18.

9. Philemon Tarnowsky, "The Ruthenians," *Immigrants in America Review* (New York: Committee for Immigrants in America, April 1916).

10. Interview with Mary Boreth, in *They Chose America: Conversations with Immigrants,* Vol. 2,

An Audio Cassette Program (Princeton, N.J.: Visual Education Corp., 1975).

11. "Five Polish Letters" in *Immigrants in America Review* (New York: Committee for Immigrants in America, April 1916), p. 60.

12. Thomas and Znaniecki, *The Polish Peasant in Europe and America,* pp. 354–355.

13. Davis, *The Russian Immigrant,* p. 202.

14. Ibid., p. 205.

15. Capek, *The Cechs in America,* p. 53.

16. Adamic, *Laughing in the Jungle,* pp. 11–12.

17. Marcus Ravage, *An American in the Making: The Life Story of an Immigrant* (1917; reprint ed., New York: Dover Publications, 1971), p. 49.

18. Thomas and Znaniecki, *The Polish Peasant in Europe and America,* p. 386.

19. Hugh Downs interview of Esther Hagler on KOED-TV, San Francisco, December 1977.

20. Miriam Kochan, *The Last Days of Imperial Russia, 1910–1917* (New York: Macmillan Publishing Co., 1976), p. 67.

21. Ibid., pp. 17–18.

Chapter 3. Shver Tsu Zayn a Yid

1. Quoted in Carl Wittke, *We Who Built America: The Saga of the Immigrant* (Englewood Cliffs, N.J.: Prentice-Hall, 1939), p. 332.

2. Chaim Potok, *Wanderings: Chaim Potok's History of the Jews* (New York: Alfred A. Knopf, 1978), p. 338.

3. Ravage, *An American in the Making,* pp. 47–48.

4. Secretary Hay's Note, reprinted in Samuel Joseph,

Jewish Immigration to the United States from 1881 to 1910 (New York: Arno Press and The New York Times, 1969), pp. 202–205.

5. Quoted in Gerard Israel, *The Jews in Russia* New York: St. Martin's Press, 1975), p. 26.

6. Maurice Samuel, *The World of Sholom Aleichem* (New York: Alfred A. Knopf, 1943), pp. 25–29.

7. Quoted in Israel, *The Jews in Russia,* p. 319.

8. Potok, *Wanderings,* p. 378.

9. Harold Frederic, *The New Exodus: A Study of Israel in Russia,* quoted in David Phillipson, *Old European Jewries* (New York: AMS Press, 1975), pp. 182–183.

10. Quoted in Howard Morley Sachar, *The Course of Modern Jewish History* (New York: Dell Publishing Co., 1977), pp. 245–246.

11. Golda Meir, *My Life* (New York: G. P. Putnam's Sons, 1975), p. 14.

12. Article published by *Novosti* 101 (April 14, 1903), quoted in Israel, *The Jews in Russia,* p. 65.

13. "Ida Richter" in Sydelle Kramer and Jenny Masur, eds., *Jewish Grandmothers* (Boston: Beacon Press, 1976), p. 64.

14. Meir, *My Life,* p. 22.

15. "The Memoirs of Dr. George M. Price," quoted in Irving Howe, *World of Our Fathers* (New York: Harcourt Brace Jovanovich, 1976), p. 27.

Chapter 4. The Taste of America

1. Mary Antin, *From Plotzk to Boston* (Boston: W. B. Clarke & Co., 1899), pp. 11–12.

2. Wytrwal, *America's Polish Heritage,* p. 37.

3. *Noviny Lipy Slovanska,* February 14, 1849,

quoted in Capek, *The Cechs in America,* pp. 33–34.

4. Quoted in Capek, *The Cechs in America,* pp. 37–38.

5. Phillip Taylor, *The Distant Magnet* (London: Eyre & Spottiswoode, 1971), p. 74.

6. Quoted in W. S. Kuniczak, *My Name is Million* (Garden City, N.Y.: Doubleday & Co., 1978), p. 70.

7. Quoted in Balch, *Our Slavic Fellow Citizens,* p. 135.

8. Quoted in Victor R. Greene, *The Slavic Community on Strike: Immigrant Labor in Pennsylvania Anthracite* (Notre Dame, Ind.: University of Notre Dame Press, 1968), p. 28.

9. Quoted in Thomas and Znaniecki, *The Polish Peasant in Europe and America,* p. 312.

10. Mary Antin, *The Promised Land* (Boston: Houghton Mifflin Co., 1912), p. 148.

11. Ibid., p. 197.

12. Stoyan Christowe, *This Is My Country* (New York: Carrick & Evans, 1938), p. 10.

13. Adamic, *Laughing in the Jungle,* pp. 3–5.

14. Kuniczak, *My Name is Million,* pp. 108–109.

Chapter 5. Departure and Arrival

1. James D. Bratush, *Historical Documentary of the Ukrainian Community of Rochester, N.Y.* (Rochester: James D. Bratush, 1973), p. xii.

2. Ravage, *An American in the Making,* pp. 51 and 55.

3. Interview with Nina Goodenov, in *They Chose America,* Vol. 1.

4. Christowe, *This Is My Country,* pp. 26–27.
5. Antin, *From Plotzk to Boston,* pp. 41–43.
6. Isaac Metzker, ed., *A Bintel Brief: Sixty Years of Letters from the Lower East Side to the Jewish Daily Forward* (New York: Ballantine Books, 1972), pp. 101–102.
7. Christowe, *This Is My Country,* p. 28.
8. Interview with Mary Marchak, in *They Chose America,* Vol. 1.
9. "Report of the International Emigration Commission," quoted in Edith Abbott, *Immigration: Select Documents and Case Records* (Chicago: University of Chicago Press, 1924), pp. 80–81.
10. "Steerage Conditions," *Reports of U.S. Immigration Commission XXXVII,* quoted in Abbott, *Immigration,* pp. 84–86.
11. Anzia Yezierska, "How I Found America," *The Century* 101, no. 1 (November 1920), p. 76.
12. Interview with Nina Goodenov, in *They Chose America,* Vol. 1.
13. Adamic, *Laughing in the Jungle,* pp. 43–44.

Chapter 6. All That Glittered Was Not Gold

1. Yezierska, "How I Found America," p. 76.
2. Oscar Handlin, *The Uprooted* (Boston: Atlantic Monthly Press, 1973), pp. 69–70.
3. Quoted in Milton Meltzer, *Bread and Roses: The Struggle of American Labor 1865–1915* (New York: Vintage Sundial Books, 1973), pp. 136–137.
4. Ibid., p. 137.
5. "Inter-Church World Movement Report on the

Steel Strike of 1919," quoted in Davis, *The Russian Immigrant,* p. 19.

6. Ibid., p. 33.
7. "Child Labor and the Welfare Children in an Anthracite Coal-Mining District," Publication no. 106, Children's Bureau, U.S. Department of Labor, quoted in Miller, *Peasant Pioneers,* p. 116.
8. Miller, *Peasant Pioneers,* p. 58.
9. Upton Sinclair, *The Jungle* (New York: The New American Library of World Literature, 1960), pp. 31–32.
10. "Report of the Massachusetts Commission on Immigration" (1914) quoted in Abbott, *Immigration,* p. 527.
11. "Child Labor and the Welfare of Children in an Anthracite Coal-Mining District," quoted in Miller, *Peasant Pioneers,* p. 117.
12. Quoted in Meltzer, *Bread and Roses,* pp. 29–30.
13. Ibid., pp. 40–41.
14. Jacob A. Riis, *How the Other Half Lives: Studies Among the Tenements of New York* (New York: Dover Publications, 1971), p. 111.
15. Ibid., p. 100.
16. Ibid., p. 100.
17. Edwin Markham, "60,000 Children in Sweatshops," *Cosmopolitan,* January 1907, reprinted in Allon Schoener, *Portal to America: The Lower East Side 1870–1925* (New York: Holt, Rinehart & Winston, 1967), pp. 162–163.
18. Quoted in Davis, *The Russian Immigrant,* p. 32.
19. Sinclair, *The Jungle,* pp. 101–102.
20. Quoted in Miller, *Peasant Pioneers,* pp. 60–62.

21. Grace Abbott, "The Chicago Employment Agency and the Immigrant Worker," quoted in Edith Abbott, *Immigration,* pp. 481–483.
22. Ernest Poole, "Task Work Bowing to Factory System," *The Outlook* (November 21, 1903, reprinted in Schoener, *Portal to America,* pp. 170–171.
23. Ravage, *An American in the Making,* pp. 62–67.
24. Interview with Mary Boreth, in *They Chose America,* Vol. 2.
25. Mary Asia Hilf, *No Time for Tears* (New York: Thomas Yoseloff, 1964), pp. 127–128.
26. Meir, *My Life,* pp. 32–34.

Chapter 7. Many Americas
1. Ravage, *An American in the Making,* pp. 60–61.
2. Mike Royko, *Boss: Richard J. Daley of Chicago,* quoted in Maldwyn A. Jones, *Destination America* (New York: Holt, Rinehart & Winston, 1976), p. 146.
3. Interview with Mary Boreth, in *They Chose America,* Vol. 2.
4. Ravage, *An American in the Making,* pp. 87–88.
5. "The Ghetto Market, Hester Street," *The New York Times* (November 14, 1897), quoted in Schoener, *Portal to America,* pp. 55–56.
6. "When the Shofar Blows," *Evening Post,* September 25, 1897, quoted in Ibid., p. 110.
7. Quoted in Frank Renkiewicz, ed., *The Poles in America 1608–1972* (Dobbs Ferry, N.Y.: Oceana Publications, 1973), p. 53.
8. Quoted in Wytrwal, *America's Polish Heritage,* pp. 169–170.

9. Interview with Mary Boreth, in *They Chose America*, Vol. 2.
10. Miller, *Peasant Pioneers*, p. 96.
11. Ibid., pp. 88–89.
12. Ibid., p. 97.
13. Adamic, *Laughing in the Jungle*, p. 107.
14. "In the East Side Cafes," *New York Tribune*, September 30, 1900, quoted in Schoener, *Portal to America*, p. 135.
15. Ravage, *An American in the Making*, pp. 146–147.
16. Hutchins Hapgood, *The Spirit of the Ghetto* (Cambridge, Mass.: The Belknap Press of Harvard University Press, 1967), pp. 113–114.
17. Metzker, *A Bintel Brief*, pp. 47–48, 65–66, 68–69.
18. Christowe, *This Is My Country*, p. 163.
19. Alice Barrows Fernandez, *United States Bureau of Education Bulletin*, no. 4 (1920), quoted in Abbott, *Immigration*, p. 557.
20. *Jewish Daily Forward*, September 8, 1905, quoted in Howe, *World of Our Fathers*, p. 266.
21. Metzker, *A Bintel Brief*, pp. 162–163.
22. Adamic, *Laughing in the Jungle*, p. 101.
23. Howe, *World of Our Fathers*, p. 645.

Chapter 8. The Labor Wars

(*Author's Note*: I have relied almost entirely on two excellent references for the accounts of the 1897 coal strike and the 1909–1910 garment strikes. These are Victor R. Greene's *The Slavic Community on Strike*, and Irving Howe's *World of Our Fathers*. These volumes are recommended highly to anyone who wishes to study these labor campaigns in further detail.)

1. Kuniczak, *My Name is Million*, p. 4.
2. Greene, *Slavic Community on Strike*, pp. 129–130.
3. Ibid, p. 130.
4. Ibid., pp. 131–132.
5. Ibid., pp. 133–134.
6. Ibid., pp. 133–136.
7. Ibid., pp. 143–144.
8. Ibid., p. 151.
9. Howe, *World of Our Fathers*, pp. 298–299.
10. Ibid., p. 299.
11. Ibid., p. 299.
12. Ibid., pp. 299–300.
13. Ibid., p. 300.
14. Ibid., p. 301.
15. Ibid., p. 306.
16. Schoener, *Portal to America*, p. 171.
17. Howe, *World of Our Fathers*, pp. 305–306.

Chapter 9. The Gates Close

1. Senator Lodge in *Congressional Record,* March 16, 1896, quoted in Abbott, *Immigration,* pp. 195–196.
2. Miller, *Peasant Pioneers,* p. 67.
3. Ibid., pp. 65–66.
4. Ibid., p. 68.
5. John Higham, *Send These To Me: Jews and Other Immigrants in Urban America* (New York: Atheneum, 1975), p. 47.
6. Madison Grant, *The Passing of the Great Race,* rev. ed. (New York: Arno Press and The New York Times, 1970), pp. 89–90.

7. *Ha-Magid* (July 3, 1891), quoted in Abraham J. Karp, ed., *Golden Door to America: The Jewish Immigrant Experience* (New York: The Viking Press, 1976), p. 95.

8. Senator Lodge in Abbott, *Immigration*, pp. 193–198.

9. Quoted in Leonard Dinnerstein and David M. Reiners, *Ethnic Americans: A History of Immigration and Assimilation* (New York: New York University Press, 1977), p. 66.

10. Jones, *Destination America*, p. 228.

11. Davis, *The Russian Immigrant*, pp. 24–25.

12. "Ida Richter" in Kramer and Masur, *Jewish Grandmothers*, p. 133.

13. "Katya Govsky" in Ibid., pp. 68–69.

14. Handlin, *The Uprooted*, p. 261.

Chapter 10. A New Dark Age in Europe

1. Quoted in Terrence Des Pres, *The Survivor* (New York: Oxford University Press, 1976), p. 83.

2. Quoted in John Thorn, Roger Lockyer, and David Smith, *A History of England* (New York: Thomas Y. Crowell, 1961), p. 533.

3. "Katya Govsky" in Kramer and Masur, *Jewish Grandmothers*, p. 65.

4. Ibid., pp. 64–66.

5. Interview with Valery Arlan, Visual Education Audio Archives, 1979.

6. Interview with Ariana Arlan, Ibid.

7. Interview with Rachel Simon, Ibid.

8. Lucy S. Davidowicz, *The War Against the Jews*

1933–1945 (New York: Holt, Rinehart & Winston, 1975), p. 17.

9. Interview with Valery Arlan, Visual Education Audio Archives, 1979.
10. Quoted in Des Pres, *The Survivor,* pp. 77–78.
11. Ibid., p. 86.
12. Ibid., p. 35.
13. Lucy S. Davidowicz, *The Jewish Presence* (New York: Harcourt Brace Jovanovich, A Harvest/HBJ Book, 1978), pp. 293–294.
14. Interview with Stephen Lemkowski, in *They Chose America,* Vol. 1.
15. Interview with Bill Glass, in *They Chose America,* Vol. 2.
16. Charles L. Mee, Jr., *Meeting at Potsdam* (New York: M. Evans, 1975), p. 244.
17. Interview with George Lavos, in *They Chose America,* Vol. 2.
18. Interview with Valery Arlan, Visual Education Audio Archives, 1979.
19. Interview with George Popescu, Ibid.
20. Interview with Ariana Arlan, Ibid.
21. *The New York Times,* September 1, 1980.

Chapter 11. Survivors and Dissidents

1. *The New York Times,* April 29, 1979, p. 4.
2. Quoted in Arthur D. Morse, *While Six Million Died* (New York: Random House, 1968), p. 140.
3. Interview with Valery Gogalack, in *They Chose America,* Vol. 1.
4. Interview with Rachel Simon, Visual Education Audio Archives, 1979.

5. Interview with Bill Glass, in *They Chose America,* Vol. 2.
6. Interview with George Lavos, Ibid.
7. Ibid.
8. Interview with Rachel Simon, Visual Education Audio Archives.
9. Maldwyn A. Jones, *Destination America,* p. 234.

Bibliography

Abbot, Edith. *Immigration: Select Documents and Case Records.* Chicago: University of Chicago Press, 1924.

Adamic, Louis. *Laughing in the Jungle: The Autobiography of an Immigrant in America.* New York: Arno Press, 1969.

Antin, Mary. *From Plotzk to Boston.* Boston: W.B. Clarke & Co., 1899.

——. *The Promised Land.* Boston: Houghton Mifflin Co., 1912.

Balch, Emily Greene. *Our Slavic Fellow Citizens.* New York: Arno Press and The New York Times, 1969.

Bratush, James D. *Historical Documentary of the Ukrainian Community of Rochester, N.Y.* Rochester: James D. Bratush, 1973.

Capek, Thomas. *The Cechs (Bohemians) in America.* Boston: Houghton Mifflin Co., 1920.

Christowe, Stoyan. *This Is My Country.* New York: Carrick & Evans, 1938.

244

Crèvecoeur, Jean de. *Letters from an American Farmer.* London: 1782, reprinted in George McMichael, ed., *Anthology of American Literature,* Vol. 1. New York: Macmillan Publishing Co., 1974.

Davidowicz, Lucy S. *The Jewish Presence.* New York: Harcourt Brace Jovanovich, A Harvest/HBJ Book, 1978.

――. *The War Against the Jews 1933–1945.* New York: Holt, Rinehart & Winston, 1975.

Davis, Jerome. *The Russian Immigrant.* New York: Arno Press and The New York Times, 1969.

Des Pres, Terrence. *The Survivor.* New York: Oxford University Press, 1976.

Dinnerstein, Leonard, and David M. Reiners. *Ethnic Americans: A History of Immigration and Assimilation.* New York: New York University Press, 1977.

"Five Polish Letters," *Immigrants in America Review.* New York: Committee for Immigrants in America, April 1916

Grant, Madison. *The Passing of the Great Race.* New York. Arno Press and The New York Times, 1970.

Greene, Victor R. *The Slavic Community on Strike: Immigrant Labor in Pennsylvania Anthracite.* Notre Dame, Ind.: University of Notre Dame Press, 1968.

Handlin, Oscar. *The Uprooted.* Boston: Atlantic Monthly Press, 1973.

Hapgood, Hutchins. *The Spirit of the Ghetto.* Cambridge, Mass.: The Belknap Press of Harvard University Press, 1967.

Hendrick, Burton J. *The Jews in America.* Garden City, N.Y.: Doubleday, Page & Co., 1923.

Higham, John. *Send These To Me: Jews and Other Immigrants in Urban America.* New York: Atheneum, 1975.

Hilf, Mary Asia. *No Time for Tears.* New York: Thomas Yoseloff, 1964.

Howe, Irving. *World of Our Fathers.* New York: Harcourt Brace Jovanovich, 1976.

Israel, Gerard. *The Jews in Russia.* New York: St. Martin's Press, 1975.

Jones, Maldwyn A. *Destination America.* New York: Holt, Rinehart & Winston, 1976.

Joseph, Samuel. *Jewish Immigration to the United States from 1881 to 1910.* New York: Arno Press and The New York Times, 1969.

Karp, Abraham J., ed. *Golden Door to America: The Jewish Immigrant Experience.* New York: The Viking Press, 1976.

Kochan, Miriam. *The Last Days of Imperial Russia, 1910–1917.* New York: Macmillan Publishing Co., 1976.

Kramer, Sydelle, and Jenny Masur, eds. *Jewish Grandmothers.* Boston: Beacon Press, 1976.

Kuniczak, W. S. *My Name Is Million.* Garden City, N.Y.: Doubleday & Co., 1978.

Lyons, Eugene. *David Sarnoff, A Biography.* New York: Harper & Row, 1966.

Masur, Jenny. *See* Kramer, Sydelle.

Mee, Charles L., Jr. *Meeting at Potsdam.* New York: M. Evans, 1975.

Meir, Golda. *My Life.* New York: G. P. Putnam's Sons, 1975.

Meltzer, Milton. *Bread and Roses: The Struggle of American Labor 1865–1915.* New York: Vintage Sundial Books, 1973.

Metzker, Isaac, ed. *A Bintel Brief: Sixty Years of Letters from the Lower East Side to the Jewish Daily Forward.* New York: Ballantine Books, 1972.

Miller, Kenneth D. *Peasant Pioneers: An Interpretation of the Slavic Peoples in the United States.* San Francisco. R & E Associates, 1969.

Morse, Arthur D. *While Six Million Died.* New York: Random House, 1968.

Pares, Bernard. *A History of Russia* New York: Vintage Books, 1965.

Phillipson, David. *Old European Jewries.* New York: AMS Press, 1975.

Potok, Chaim. *Wanderings: Chaim Potok's History of the Jews.* New York: Alfred A. Knopf, 1978.

Prpic, George J. *The Croatian Immigrants in America.* New York: Philosophical Library, 1971.

Ravage, Marcus. *An American in the Making: The Life Story of an Immigrant.* New York: Dover Publications, 1971.

Renkiewicz, Frank, ed. *The Poles in America 1608–1972.* Dobbs Ferry, N.Y.: Oceana Publications, 1973.

Riis, Jacob A. *How the Other Half Lives: Studies Among the Tenements of New York.* New York: Dover Publications, 1971.

Sachar, Howard Morley. *The Course of Modern Jewish History.* New York: Dell Publishing Co., 1977.

Samuel, Maurice. *The World of Sholom Aleichem.* New York: Alfred A. Knopf, 1943.

Schoener, Allon. *Portal to America: The Lower East Side 1870–1925.* New York: Holt, Rinehart & Winston, 1967.

Sinclair, Upton. *The Jungle.* New York: The New American Library of World Literature, 1960.

Tarnowsky, Philemon. "The Ruthenians," *Immigrants in America Review.* New York: Committee for Immigrants in America, April 1916.

Taylor, Phillip. *The Distant Magnet.* London: Eyre & Spottiswoode, 1971.

They Chose America: Conversations with Immigrants. Vols. 1 and 2. An Audio Cassette Program. Princeton, N.J.: Visual Education Corp., 1975.

Thomas, William L., and Florian Znaniecki, *The Polish Peasant in Europe and America.* Vol. 1. New York: Octagon Books, 1974.

Thorn, John, Roger Lockyer, and David Smith. *A History of England.* New York: Thomas. Y. Crowell, 1961.

Warriner, Doreen. *Contrasts in Emerging Societies.* Bloomington: Indiana University Press, 1965.

Wilson, Woodrow. *A History of the American People,* Vol. 5. New York: Harper & Bros., 1902.

Wittke, Carl. *We Who Built America: The Saga of the Immigrant.* Englewood Cliffs, N.J.: Prentice-Hall, 1939.

Wytrwal, Joseph A. *America's Polish Heritage: A Social History of the Poles in America.* Detroit: Endurance Press, 1961.

Yezierska, Anzia. "How I Found America," *The Century* 101, no. 1, November 1920.

A Brief History of U.S. Immigration Laws

The authority to formulate immigration policy rests with Congress and is contained in Article 1, Section 8, Clause 3 of the Constitution, which provides that Congress shall have the power to "regulate commerce with foreign nations, and among the several States, and with the Indian tribes."

Alien Act of 1798: authorized the deportation of aliens by the President. Expired after two years.

For the next seventy-five years there was no federal legislation restricting admission to, or allowing deportation from, the United States.

Act of 1875: excluded criminals and prostitutes and entrusted inspection of immigrants to collectors of the ports.

Act of 1882: excluded lunatics and idiots and persons liable to becoming public charges.

First Chinese Exclusion Act.

Acts of 1885 and 1887: contract labor laws, which made it unlawful to import aliens under contract for labor or services of any kind. (Exceptions: artists, lecturers, servants, skilled aliens in an industry not yet established in the United States, etc.)

249

Act of 1888: amended previous acts to provide for expulsion of aliens landing in violation of contract laws.

Act of 1891: first exclusion of persons with certain diseases; felons, also persons having committed crimes involving moral turpitude; polygamists, etc.

Act of 1903: further exclusion of persons with certain mental diseases, epilepsy, etc; beggars; also "anarchists or persons who believe in, or advocate the overthrow by force or violence of the Government of the United States or of all government or of all forms of law or the assassination of public officials." Further refined deportation laws.

Acts of 1907, 1908: further exclusions for health reasons, such as tuberculosis.

Exclusion of persons detrimental to labor conditions in the United States, specifically Japanese and Korean skilled or unskilled laborers.

Gentlemen's Agreement with Japan: in which Japan agreed to restrictions imposed by the United States.

Act of 1917: codified previous exclusion provisions, and added literacy test. Further restricted entry of other Asians.

Act of 1921: First Quota Law, in which approximately 350,000 immigrants were permitted entry, mostly from northern or western Europe.

Act of 1924: National Origins Quota System set annual limitations on the number of aliens of any nationality immigrating to the U.S. The act also decreed, in a provision aimed primarily at the Japanese, that no alien ineligible for citizenship could be admitted to the U.S.

"Gigolo Act" of 1937: allowing deportation of aliens fraudulently marrying in order to enter the United States either by having marriage annulled or by refusing to marry once having entered the country.

Act of 1940: Alien Registration Act provided for registration and fingerprinting of all aliens.

Act of 1943: Chinese Exclusion Acts repealed.

Act of 1945: War Brides Act admitted during the three years of act's existence approximately 118,000 brides, grooms, and children of servicemen who had married foreign nationals during World War II.

Act of 1949: Displaced Persons Act admitted more than four hundred thousand people displaced as a result of World War II (to 1952).

Act of 1950: Internal Security Act excluded from immigrating any present or foreign member of the Communist party, and made more easily deportable people of this class already in the U.S. Also provided for alien registration by January 10 of each year.

Act of 1952: Immigration and Nationality Act codified all existing legislation; also eliminated race as a bar to immigration.

Acts of 1953–1956: Refugee Relief acts admitted orphans, Hungarians after 1956 uprising, skilled sheepherders.

1957: special legislation to admit Hungarian refugees.

1960: special legislation paroled Cuban refugees into the U.S.

Act of 1965: legislation amending act of 1952 phased out national origins quotas by 1968, with new numerical ceilings on a first come, first served basis. Numerical ceilings (per annum): 120,000 for natives of the Western Hemisphere; 170,000 for natives of the Eastern Hemisphere. New preference categories: relatives (74 percent), scientists, artists (10 percent), skilled and unskilled labor (10 percent), refugees (6 percent).

Act of 1977: allowed Indo-Chinese who had been paroled into the U.S. to adjust their status to permanent resident.

1979: Presidential directive allowed thousands of Vietnamese "boat people" to enter the U.S.

1980: Presidential directive allowed some 125,000 Cubans to enter the U.S. as political refugees.

Index

253